Shrop

Telford & the Ironbridge Gorge

Judy Smith

For our granddaughter Amber. You can see the Shropshire Hills on your horizon. We hope that you will be able to enjoy this lovely county at closer quarters one day.

Thanks are due to:

Eric, who also loves to explore Shropshire, but was often obliged to stay at home 'puppy-sitting'. I am very grateful.

The staff of Tourist Offices throughout the county, and all the other helpful individuals I met in my travels.

Above: The Wrekin from Grinshill

Below: Pitchford Hall

Shropshire

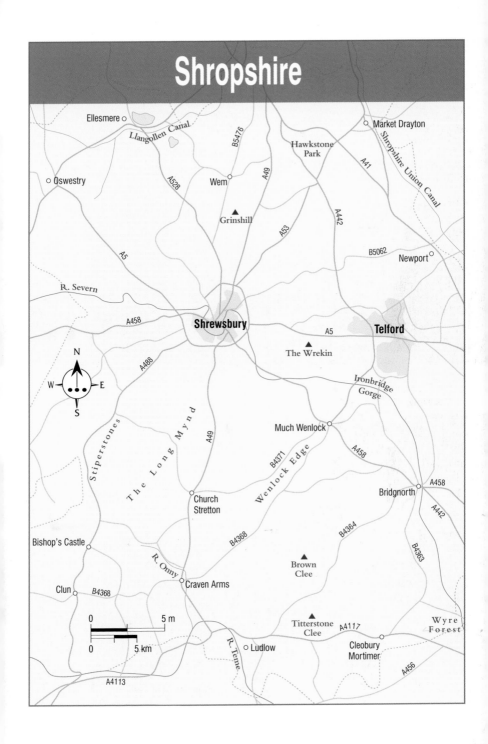

Contents

This book will take you on a journey through Shropshire – beside the sandy banks of the Severn, over the varied hills of the south, along the towpaths and waterways of the north, through the medieval streets and alleyways of its county town. Ancient churches and abbeys are explored, as are prehistoric trackways, industrial heritage sites, stately homes, restored railways and all the many other facets of this delightful county.

Shropshire is splendidly rich and diverse, with plenty of interest for everyone. Geologists claim the county to be unique in that rocks from every era of time can be found here. Many of the most interesting geological sites have been endowed with information panels so that the novice as well as the expert can appreciate them. For historians there are prehistoric megaliths, Iron Age hill forts, Norman churches and a string of ruined castles along the Welsh

Top Tips

1) The Llangollen Canal. At least take a walk beside it, but a week's narrowboating holiday is better!

2) The half-timbered buildings and medieval 'shuts' of Shrewsbury.

3) The hilly horizon. Climb Stiperstones, the Long Mynd, Brown Clee, the Wrekin or Corndon for a breathtaking prospect (even Grinshill or Lyth Hill will do)

4) Bridgnorth. Take a ride on the unique cliff railway and enjoy a royal view.

5) Time-warped Clun. Sit beside the packhorse bridge and slip back through the centuries.

6) The Ironbridge Gorge. The story told in its museums is fascinating.

7) The Secret Hills Discovery Centre - packed with local information and suggestions for adventures outdoors.

8) The peaceful Mere at Ellesmere. Take a steamboat trip and soak up the atmosphere of the 1930s

9) The Severn Valley Railway. Enjoy splendid prospects of the river along with the magic of steam.

10) Ludlow - the castle, the streets, the shops and simply everything about this 'loveliest town in England'

border. Elsewhere are tales of Clive of India, the fugitive Charles II, Thomas Telford, Charles Darwin and of course, Abraham Darby and his revolutionary method for the smelting of coal. Walkers of all abilities have a paradise in the rolling landscapes of the Shropshire Hills, and cyclists can enjoy a network of waymarked trails throughout the county. 'Foodies' will essentially find themselves in gustatory heaven with Shropshire's devotion to local produce and festivals of food and drink. And for those with a literary bent, there is the countryside so atmospherically described in the novels of Mary Webb, the Shrewsbury Abbey of Ellis Peter's Cadfael stories, and memorials to war poet Wilfred Owen in his home town of Oswestry and in Shrewsbury. In the south-west, the poignant words penned by A E Housman in *A Shropshire Lad* are brought to life with every turn of the road. No other English county has merited a whole suite of poetry devoted to it!

The Shropshire of this book has been divided into five geographical areas, and unlike many other travel guides, all the information given is linked by location rather than alphabetically. Hopefully this will make it not only a practical travel guide but a book that can enjoyed by the fireside on a winter's night. With that in mind, all the background information and other incidental stories are to be found in the place where they naturally occur. More specific information like the opening times and telephone numbers of the places you might like to visit can be found at the end of each chapter. Here too can be found suggestions for walks and cycle rides, and a few recommendations for family outings. Finally there are ideas for what to do on a rainy day – and since this book was made in the summer of 2008, they are offered with a certain amount of authority! Extra information at the back of the book includes teashops and inns for refreshment, swimming pools, golf courses, equestrian establishments, market days, major annual events, and more.

If you are visiting Shropshire for the first time, I hope you will find in these pages all that you need to pack your holiday with interest. If, like me, you are lucky enough to live in or near the county and think you know it well - maybe even so you will be able to discover something new. I hope that you will have as much pleasure from this book as I have had in making it and that it tempts you to spend many happy days exploring Shropshire. Good luck on your journey!

Judy Smith

1. Wetlands and Waterways
– the North of the County

North of Shrewsbury the countryside is low-lying, a rolling landscape of red-brick farmhouses and lush fields grazed by black and white cattle. At the centre of this area, the vast expanse of peat marsh and lakes known as the 'mosses and meres' now boasts several nature reserves that are unique in Europe. And through it all meanders the Llangollen Canal, that most attractive and popular of inland waterways, while its 'parent' Shropshire Union Canal nips through just ten miles of the county on its eastern border. This is rural England at its very best, and the five old market towns scattered across it each have their own individual character and a story to tell

The Border Land

Like reading the written page, this journey through Shropshire begins at the top left-hand corner – or perhaps in this case it would be better to say the north-west tip. Here on the Welsh border is a scene not to be missed – the railway and Llangollen Canal make their entry into Shropshire side

Aqueduct and viaduct over the Ceiriog

by side on high-arched viaduct and aqueduct spanning the valley of the River Ceiriog near Chirk. Below them Telford's old A5 coach road arrives rather less dramatically by means of a simple stone bridge. It is possible to walk over the aqueduct (and, should you be feeling brave, on into 'Darkie' tunnel beyond) – on the Shropshire side of the road bridge, turn right (SP Chirk Bank) to a parking area beside the canal and from there simply follow the towpath.

From Chirk Bank, both road and railway are heading for Shrewsbury – and the canal would have been too,

High Drama

Built around 1800, ten-arched Chirk Aqueduct crosses the River Ceiriog (the border with Wales) at a height of 70 feet. Both Telford and Jessop had a hand in its design. Some 50 years after its construction, the parallel 30-feet higher railway viaduct was added by Scottish engineer Henry Robertson. Unfortunately these impressive feats of engineering are often overlooked because just a couple of miles further down the canal the more famous 126 feet high Poncysyllte Aqueduct vaults the valley of the Dee.

but that's another story. Instead it turns east and through its twisting winding journey, provides by far the best introduction to this northern part of Shropshire. But to follow it immediately would be to miss the first of the market towns, Oswestry, just five miles south down the A5.

Taking that road towards Oswestry, you soon pass (on the left) **Park Hall** Estate. The original fine Tudor house burnt down in 1918 and the remaining premises were used as a military camp from World War II onwards. Today Park Hall is a real working farm that welcomes visitors, giving children the opportunity to handle the animals, feed the lambs and milk the cows. With mini tractors to ride, diggers to work, small animals to cuddle and a lot more, a whole day should be reserved for the visit.

Almost opposite Park Hall, the curious flat-topped mound on the right of the A5 is **Hen Dinas**, one of the most extensive Iron Age hill forts in the country. Ringed by three or four layers of ramparts, it is so large that it takes some 20 minutes to walk the track that runs around its flat central dwelling area. From this summit path, ramparts, ditches and two entrances can be seen quite clearly and the 360 degree vista takes in the Breiddens and the Shropshire Hills, as well as the more distant Welsh hills to the north. Legend has it that Queen Guinevere was born at Hen Dinas – Shropshire joins with most of the Celtic world in claiming connections with the King Arthur saga. To reach the hill fort, simply follow the brown signs as you approach the town. There is parking beside the main entrance gate, and information panels have recently been installed.

Oswestry

Oswestry is the third largest town in Shropshire and since earliest times has been important for its market, where Welsh hill farmers mingle with those from the plains below. The town's rather curious name derives from the events of the nearby Battle of Maserfield in 641AD. It was here that Penda, the pagan King of Mercia slew Oswald, the Christian King of Northumbria, and then dismembered his body as a lesson to others who might threaten his rule. The story goes that a passing eagle swooped down and carried the severed arm to a tree, and 'Oswald's Tree' became 'Oswestry'. When the arm finally dropped to the ground a spring burst forth, and it can still be visited today as 'St Oswald's Well' (near the church).

The earliest evidence of settlement on the site of Oswestry is the remains of an 11th century castle close to the present day shopping area. A well-kept grassy mound is all that is now to be seen, but this castle was once important in Edward I's defence of the Welsh border and later as a Royalist stronghold in the Civil War. A walk to the top of Castle Bank offers a splendid view over the town.

Oswestry's cattle market has now moved out of town, and the central square that was once its home has been invested with a bronze statue of a shepherd and his sheep. In the surrounding shopping streets, bright latter-day facades contrast oddly with the handful of half-timbered buildings lingering from a previous age. Carved and beamed Llwyd Mansion, dating from 1604 and now housing a chic hairdressing salon on its ground floor, is a classic example!

Oswestry strangely has two Tourist Information Centres. The one on the east side goes under the name of the Cambrian Visitor Centre and is housed in the old railway station. It tells the story of Oswestry's former role as the headquarters of the railway network serving North and mid-Wales and is something of a taster for what is around the corner. An old railway shed now shelters the Cambrian Railway Museum, a hotch-potch of rolling stock, bits of engines and other railway memorabilia for which there is no entrance fee and no set opening hours. Most days and most afternoons at least there will be someone on hand to share his knowledge and his enthusiasm.

The second and perhaps slightly better stocked Information Centre is at the other end of the town, close to St Oswald's church, with its handsome Norman tower. In Broad Walk beside the church, a large plaque commemorates World War I poet Wilfred Owen, born in Oswestry in 1893. The Tourist Information Centre can be found across the churchyard from Broad Walk, where it occupies the premises of an early 15th century Grammar School, said to be the second oldest such in England. Under the sagging roof beams, a tiny room houses the Information Centre, while the remaining space is devoted to an attractive coffee shop.

Wilfred Owen

Wilfred Owen, the oldest of four children, was born in March 1893 at his grandparents' Oswestry home, Plas Wilmot. The large house is just off the Welshpool road – devotees could ask Tourist Information for directions. The family subsequently moved around and finally settled in Shrewsbury when Owen was 13.

Although writing poetry from an early age, it was his meeting with Siegfried Sassoon at a military hospital in Edinburgh that inspired him to his best and most poignant war poems. Wilfred Owen was tragically killed in the final week of the war, his parents receiving news of his death as the nation celebrated the armistice. Sadly only five of his poems had been published at the time and his acclaim was largely achieved posthumously. Interest in Owen was revived when Benjamin Britten used several of his texts alongside the Latin Mass for the Dead in his War Requiem, commissioned for the consecration of the new Coventry Cathedral in 1962.

Spoonerisms

Another of Oswestry's sons was the Rev. William Archibald Spooner, born in 1844 and renowned for his amusing confusion of consonants and syllables. His attributed faux pas include a loyal toast to the 'queer old Dean' and the observation that 'it is kisstomary to cuss the bride', but the Tourist Board is even more delighted with his professed 'Shove of Lopshire'. (Did he really utter that one?)

Oswestry, Llwyd Mansion

South of Oswestry are a collection of nature reserves owned by Shropshire Wildlife Trust. All can be visited (leaflets from any Tourist Information) and all offer an interesting mix of plant and animal life, but at Llynclys Common and Llanymynech Rocks you will also find sections of the long earthwork known as **Offa's Dyke**. Built by the 8th century King of Mercia, the whole bank stretched from near Chepstow in the south to Prestatyn in the north, a distance of around 180 miles along the Welsh border. Whether it was designed simply as a boundary marker or had a more defensive role is still in debate. Llanymynech Rocks is also the site of an old limestone quarry, and in the scree it is possible to find fossils of corals and other shells that prove the area was once under the sea.

Back to Oswestry now, and the best way to return to the canal is via the Ellesmere road, on the way passing through the village of **Whittington**. Yes, it does claim to have been the home of the legendary Dick – see the box – but for the moment just stop on the

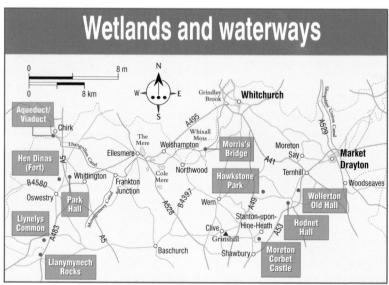

Turn again, Whittington

Dick Whittington was the third son of Sir William Whittington of Pauntley in Gloucestershire, but despite this, Shropshire has it that he spent his childhood years living in Whittington Castle. Certainly he married Alice, the daughter of Sir Ivo FitzWarine, who owned Whittington Castle in the 14th century. Adding weight to Shropshire's assertions is the well-known fact that Dick Whittington 'turned again' on Highgate Hill. He would never have been going home that way if he was living in Gloucestershire!

Celtic Cross and Visitor Centre, Oswestry

Whittington Castle

roadside and admire the twin entrance towers of its 12th century castle, perfectly reflected in the tranquil moat below. The pair of swans that have adopted this as their home add to the scene! No one knows how long there has been a castle in Whittington, but the first structure in stone was built by William Peverell, a son of William the Conqueror. After the male line of Peverells died out, the Fitz-Warine family took over the castle and substantially added to its fortifications. In occupation until the Civil War, it was afterwards plundered for its stone. The tide of its fortunes has now turned – in 1998 the villagers of Whittington formed the Whittington Castle Preservation Trust to take over the care of their fortress on a 99-year lease. This is the only community-owned castle in England! If you have a few moments, park in the carpark alongside, go in and admire the restoration work, and perhaps enjoy a cuppa in the little tea-shop – all contributions are ploughed back into the maintenance of this handsome medieval site.

The Llangollen Canal passes just to the north of Whittington through the village of **Hindford** and then creeps eastwards between fields of grazing cattle to reach a junction at the hamlet of Lower Frankton. From here the Montgomery Canal drops through four locks before continuing to its 'dead end' eight miles to the south, while the main line winds on to Ellesmere. Nowadays this junction is a picturesque and peaceful scene (and you can park at the picnic site on the road south of Welsh Frankton to admire it) but it was not designed to be so. This little-used **Montgomery Canal** should have

13

The Llangollen Canal

There was never a plan to build the 'Llangollen Canal'. Instead a waterway joining the Mersey to the Severn was envisaged, and in 1793 work began on the section from Chester to the north and, in the middle of the countryside, an isolated branch to Llanymynech quarry. The latter was extended, but never got nearer to Shrewsbury than Weston Lullingfields, while in the north, although the Pontcysyllte aqueduct had been completed, progress was halted by Ruabon Mountain. Money was short and the cost of cutting through or locking over the mountain was enormous. It was decided to extend five more miles to Llangollen to obtain a supply of water from the Dee, and to connect the existing canal to the Chester Canal at Hurleston (near Nantwich).

The present day canal is therefore a compromise – and a happy one! It survived the 1968 act abandoning many canals because it supplied (and still does) the water for Crewe, and with the advent of leisure boating, it has become the most popular of all Britain's inland waterways. Highlights include the locks at Grindley Brook, Whixall Moss, the meres around Ellesmere and the aqueducts at Chirk and Pontcysyllte. With a journey time of around 20 hours from Hurleston to Llangollen it is possible to explore the whole canal in a week's holiday. Listed below are some of the boat hire bases that offer that opportunity.

Alvechurch Boat Centre*, Wrenbury. ☎ 01270 780544.
Viking Afloat, Whitchurch. ☎ 01948 662012
Blackwater Meadow Marina*, Ellesmere. ☎ 01691 624391
Maestermyn Marine, Whittington. ☎ 01691 662424
Chirk Marina*, Whitehurst, Chirk. ☎ 01691 774558
Anglo-Welsh Canal Wharf*, Trevor. ☎ 01978 821749
* denotes added possibility of day boat hire

been the main route to Shrewsbury, busy with cargo boats – but canal planning seldom worked out as intended, and nowhere is this more evident than on the Llangollen.

Ellesmere

Just 3 road miles from Frankton Junction is the delightful town of Ellesmere. Ellesmere is at the heart of Shropshire's 'Lake District', a lovely old market town well worth a visit. Among its elegant Georgian houses and black and white half-timbered buildings are some interesting craft and antique shops and an irresistible delicatessen-cum-bakery by the name of Vermeulen's. Just behind the town centre, a long arm of canal leads up to the former wharf, its crane and old warehouse gaunt reminders of time past. At present (2008) a new development is being undertaken around this wharf. Can it possibly complement the scene?

Canal centre it may have been, but Ellesmere's main attraction is the large lake to the east of the town. Known simply as 'The Mere', it is the largest and deepest of many such stretches of water – nearby are Blake Mere, Cole Mere, White Mere, Newton Mere and several more. The Mere itself seems little changed since the 1930s, when then owner Lord Brownlow built his boathouse beside it, and the stately Wellingtonias and abundant rhododendrons of Cremorne Gardens were all part of his estate. In 1953, both Mere and gardens were generously given for public use. Today there are wooden rowing boats for hire, and a classic steamboat takes passengers around the water. A Visitor Centre near the boathouse gives the history of the 'mosses and meres', and also carries a wealth of information on the birdlife (including a video link with the local heronry). In 2008 there are plans to combine the Visitor Centre and Boathouse into one building – hopefully the between-the-wars character of this waterside will be faithfully retained.

Ellesmere has one other site to explore. Between Mere and canal, the long wooded mound is a natural glacial moraine and in the 11th century, local landowner Roger de Montgomerie built a motte and bailey on the site. Today paths wind through the woodland to complete a gentle mile-and-a-half walk that includes the best of all Ellesmere's watery scenes!

The canal sees the best of this countryside, and to the east of Ellesmere it runs beside the shores of lovely Blake Mere. A mile or so farther on, **Cole Mere** sparkles through the trees on the opposite bank – the lake and surrounding woodland form a Country Park (reached by car from the A528)

that offers a pleasant mile-long circular walk.

None of the other meres is as accessible as Cole Mere, but in a few more twists and turns, the canal brings you conveniently to the edge of **Whixall Moss**. Access by car is more complicated – take the A495 as far as **Welshampton** (its church with a patterned slate roof was designed by Sir Gilbert Scott), and there turn right where signed to Wem. In the village of Northwood, brown signs to Whixall NNR take you on through Dobson's Bridge and over Morris's lift bridge to a small car park on the edge of the Moss. Free information booklets are available from the box beside the canal here, and you can walk up the wide grassy track, passing the site of an old peat mill, to join the official Mosses Trail. This circular route of 4 miles (including 1½ miles on the canal towpath) should give you a feel for this atmospheric lowland, where white cotton grass dances beside the brackish water, and sparse colonies of silver birch break the flat horizon. Wandering off the trail is not recommended, but there are one or two other rights of way across the moss, extending to the area known as Fenn's Moss in the north.

Leaving Morris's Bridge, once again the canal has the easiest passage, reaching Whitchurch in 5 fairly direct miles, while the road winds through never-ending fields of plump Friesian cattle, and negotiates innumerable off-the-beaten-track junctions.

Whitchurch

Whitchurch is the oldest continuously inhabited settlement in Shropshire. The Romans called it Mediolanum,

Mosses, Meres and Moraines

About 25,000 years ago, huge glaciers flowing down from the mountains of Wales and the Lake District covered low-lying Shropshire with ice. As the glaciers retreated, they left a debris of sand and gravel on the underlying New Red Sandstone. When the retreat slowed, the debris was piled, causing the hummocks known as moraines; and where pockets of ice remained in the debris, these finally melted to form meres. No stream flows in or out of these meres – they each have a bed of clay, and maintain their level by natural seepage from the surrounding countryside.

Since a mere has no outflow, dead vegetation accumulates in its bed and eventually fills it. In time this decomposing mass rises above the water and forms a peat bog, colonised by acid-loving plants – a 'moss' in local parlance. Commercial peat digging was practised on these mosses until some 20 years ago. Today the largest moss (Whixall) is a National Nature Reserve and others are protected sites.

the town mid-way between Wroxeter (Shrewsbury) and Chester, while later on it became Westune to the Saxons and then Album Monasterium to the Normans. As latter-day Whitchurch, its fame largely rests on the work of J B Joyce, a firm making tower clocks that became established in the town in 1690 and still has its premises on the outskirts. Joyce's clocks are to be found all over the world (as far afield as Kabul and Singapore), but Whitchurch retains half a dozen models scattered throughout the town, and shows off the workings of one in its Heritage Centre.

Whitchurch is justly proud of that Heritage Centre (just off the High Street). In addition to the clock model there are various other displays and an abundance of literature relating to the area. For such a small town (population 9,000) Whitchurch seems very

strong on 'trails' – the Clock Trail is an obvious choice, but there is also a Discovery Trail, an Edward German Trail, a Mosaic Trail, a Family Fun Trail, a Town Mouse Trail and quite possibly others! Most trails lead up the High Street, where among the shops there are one or two attractive half-timbered buildings, and every trail includes a visit to the town's most prominent edifice, the Church of St Alkmund, at the top of the hill. The original church here was built over a Roman ditch, causing the tower to collapse dramatically one Sunday evening in 1711, fortunately after the congregation had left! If you visit the present building (built on firmer foundations two years later), look out for a coffin-shaped stone in the church porch. Beneath it lies the heart of John Talbot, Earl of Shrewsbury, immortalised by Shakespeare in Henry

VI Part I (the rest of him was brought back to Whitchurch some 50 years later, and is buried in the south aisle).

On the outskirts of Whitchurch, the Llangollen Canal is again the most interesting feature. A long arm of it reaches towards the town, and the Tourist Board dreams of a day when enough money will have been raised to build an inclined plane, and visiting boats will be magically lifted to moor in the heart of town. In the meantime, the most exciting watery scene is at **Grindley Brook**, just a mile north of town, where six locks drop the canal 40 feet to leave Shropshire for the plains of Cheshire. The first three of these locks form a 'staircase' – that is, the bottom gate of the first is also the top gate of the second and so on down the

Oswestry Market Shepherd

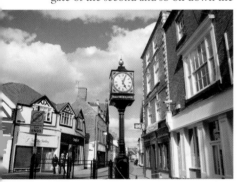
J B Joyce clock in central Whitchurch

Church at Welshampton

Edward German (1862 – 1936)

Edward German was born Edward German Jones, the son of a Whitchurch publican who was also church organist. The family lived at the Cornmarket Inn off the High Street, an establishment now known as the Old Town Hall Vaults – if you visit it today, you will find old photographs and memorabilia on the walls. While still in Whitchurch, German organised a local band, learned the piano and organ, and taught himself the violin. Later educated more formally at the Royal Academy, he became musical director at the Globe Theatre, where he wrote popular incidental music to the plays. After being asked to complete Sullivan's unfinished opera 'the Emerald Isle', German went on to write his own operettas, of which 'Merrie England' is possibly the most renowned. He was knighted in 1928.

Edward German is buried in the cemetery on Mile Bank Road (the road to Marbury), where his grave is signposted.

line. This arrangement makes for rapid descent (or ascent), but is not that easy to operate, as you can see from the board giving boaters their instructions. At Grindley Brook a lock keeper is usually on duty to keep everyone in order and also to ensure maximum conservation of water. Even so, things do not always run smoothly, and the outdoor tables of the café alongside make the perfect vantage point from which to watch the fun.

Wem

At Grindley Brook the Llangollen Canal disappears into Cheshire. Leave it to go and instead turn south to the next of the market towns, Wem. Its curious name means 'marsh', and indeed Wem sits among low-lying fields along the banks of the River Roden. At first glance it seems an unremarkable place (most of its original buildings were destroyed by a fire in 1677), but there are some very good reasons for a pause in Wem. Do you believe there is such a thing as a treacle mine? Several places lay claim to one, but in Wem it was possibly the mixed effluent from the brewery and adjacent slaughterhouse - or maybe the chemist's residue of molasses - that once made the place run thick, black and sticky. Today Wem's 'Treacle Mine' is a tiny shop in the main street selling a wonderful variety of colourful sweets and choco-lates, all stacked in old-fashioned glass jars around the walls. Somehow they manage to fit a café in there as well.

Just along the road from the Treacle Mine is another good reason for a visit – Wem has a storytelling museum. Pop into the old library any time it is open (mostly afternoons) and someone will spin you a yarn – maybe a piece of local Shropshire folklore, maybe a tale from the Brazilian rainforest, maybe a story from the Romany heritage, maybe a classic of ancient Egypt. Various set-tings provide the appropriate backdrop, and there are fascinating artefacts like the Indian story-telling box and the South American gourd intricately en-graved with a legend. Story-telling is an art to be treasured and the Society for Storytelling Reference Library is housed in the museum. 'Mythstories' is a registered charity run by the friendly couple who established it, and there is no entry fee, only an opportunity for donation.

A short drive from Wem

Wem is surrounded by some interesting countryside that warrants at least this short excursion. Leave Wem heading east, and turn right immediately after crossing the railway line. After passing through Aston and crossing the River Roden twice, the next village you reach is pretty **Lee Brockhurst**, nes-tling at the foot of a wooded sandstone outcrop. From the little car park near the river bridge, paths lead steeply to the top of the slope, from where there are fine views across the Roden valley. This attractive little corner is now cared for by the National Trust under the name of **Lee Hills**. After leaving Lee Brockhurst on the main road (north) and turning right, winding Booley Lane will bring you to the village of **Stanton-upon-Hine Heath**, home of novelist Mary Webb (see P36) for six years between 1896 and 1902. The lovely sandstone church in the village is always open and an old sundial perches on the bank outside.

A mile down the road from Stanton, the ruins of once-elegant **Moreton Corbet Castle** stand out above the flat fields. The first fortress was built here by Bartholomew Torret just after the Norman Conquest, and, having passed through marriage into the hands of the Corbet family, a manor house was added alongside in the 16th century. Today the roofless ruins still display some of the rich classical decoration, and the always-open site has been provided with information boards that recount its story.

West of Moreton Corbet (across the B5063), a minor road leads to the A49. Just beyond that road is the last place on this tour, **Grinshill** – and though the village is interesting, the hill itself is more so. No more than a mere 630feet in height, Grinshill nevertheless has a king-sized view. From its summit plateau, Stiperstones, the Long Mynd and all the Shropshire ranges grace the southern horizon, with the wild Berwyns and Arans away in the west and the low Peckfortons to the north. A toposcope has been installed to identify them all. The summit of Grinshill is easily accessible from the village of Clive (take the path beside the church) or from the parking area at Corbet Wood (drive ¾ mile east from Clive, then turn right where signed).

If you walk or drive around the foot of Grinshill you may well see evidence of its quarries. Grinshill is a sandstone outcrop like others in this area, but it harbours a unique vein of creamy-beige sandstone that is of a particularly hard

consistency. The changes are thought to be the result of high temperatures associated with volcanic activity. Grinshill sandstone has found its way into some high places – notably Shrewsbury Abbey, Chequers, and the door surrounds and lintels of 10, Downing Street. The rock here has also yielded some interesting fossils, among them reptile footprints from the Triassic Age.

Back to Wem again now, and just 5 miles to the east, Grinshill white sandstone is at its most spectacular at the curious **Hawkstone Park Follies**. Hawkstone claims to be this country's first theme park. In the 18th century, Rowland Hill, then owner of Hawkstone estate, began creating a fantastic landscape of caves, arches, bridges and walkways in the rugged hillsides of his own grounds, which then he opened to the public. Samuel Johnson visited in 1774 and reported 'striking scenes and terrifick grandeur'. After many years of neglect, Hill's eccentric world was restored and reopened in 1993. Highlights today include the spooky labyrinth of mine tunnels, the wobbly Swiss Bridge spanning an 80ft chasm, and the climb to the top of the monument, from which – on the clearest of days - 13 counties are in view. It is advised that you bring a torch with you to explore Hawkstone – and reserve at least 3 hours to do it justice. Refreshments and do-it-yourself picnic tables are available on site.

From Hawkstone the road to the east winds through a particularly attractive valley to the village of Hodnet. Beside the road junction, **Hodnet Hall** boasts 63 acres of landscaped garden, the creation and pride of the Heber-Percy

'A rose by any other name'

Wem's other claim to fame is that it is the Home of the Sweet Pea - local resident Henry Eckford developed the plant here in 1888. For most of the year there is not much evidence of his achievement, but come to Wem on the third weekend in July and the scent could greet you a mile away! The Wem Sweet Pea Festival is a treat for eyes and noses alike!

Moreton Corbet Castle

family. Ornamental pools, waterfalls, woodland walks and formal gardens contribute to its reputation as one of England's finest gardens. Sadly it is only open to the public on a few days each year.

Gardens of a rather different nature are to be found just north of Hodnet, at Wollerton, just off the Market Drayton road (A53). Set around a 16th century house, the 4 acres of **Wollerton Old Hall Gardens** manifest formal design and particularly focus on colour and texture provided by perennials. Opening hours are a little more liberal than at Hodnet, so with care it should be possible to arrange a visit to both on the same day.

The Treacle Mine, Wem

Lock and teashop, Grindley Brook

Market Drayton

At Market Drayton you have reached canal country again – this time it is the Shropshire Union that passes to the east of the town, and there is a fine walk along the towpath to the locks in Tyrley cutting, a couple of miles down the line. But first of all, take a look at the centre of town, where the black and white half-timbered buildings seem more in keeping with the clattering of coaches and horses than the buzz of 21st century traffic. The Clive and Coffyne Inn, the next door Tudor House and the nearby Crown Inn are all survivors of the town's great fire of 1651.

Market Drayton's most famous son was Robert Clive - Clive of India - who was born at Styche Hall (in nearby Moreton Say) in 1725. He seems hardly to have been an asset to the town, as there are stories of him scaling the church tower to perch on the gargoyles and running a protection racket among the shops of the High Street.

Just possibly it was the spices that Clive brought back from India that led to Market Drayton's present day reputation as the home of gingerbread. Made from a secret recipe containing rum, the local people insist that it is at its best when also dunked in port! One Market Drayton delicacy that certainly is attributable to Clive is a sort of cotton reel-shaped pie, made from minced mutton, suet, brown sugar and lemon zest – the forerunner of today's mince pie. You may have trouble finding a 'Clive Pie' in Market Drayton, but there are plenty of them in the twin town of Pézenas in the Languedoc, where a Confraternity of Bakers is devoted to its production!

And finally back to the canal again. The **Shropshire Union** came into being in 1845 as a result of the amalgamation of four existing canals, all largely built to the designs of Thomas Telford. Telford preferred to negotiate the contours by creating embankments and cuttings, reserving locks as a last resort. The section south of Market Drayton demonstrates this perfectly, with one of the deepest of all canal cuttings beyond the Tyrley locks at Woodseaves. So thick is the vegetation here that boats moving through say they have an 'African Queen' sensation.

Before leaving this part of the county you might like to check out one more local assertion. Get a road map of Britain and draw a rectangle incorporating the most northerly, westerly, southerly and easterly points of England (including the Scilly Isles). Its diagonals should cross – at Woodseaves!

Tyrley Wharf, Market Drayton

Clive of India (1725 – 1774)

Robert Clive was born the first child of a Shropshire landowning family. After a turbulent adolescence in which he was expelled from three schools, Clive was sent by his disenchanted father to be a clerk in the East India Company. There he became embroiled in the Anglo-French conflicts, and joining a private army, proved himself a brave and capable leader. He returned to England in triumph, but soon felt the call of India again. This time the Nawab of Bengal had seized Calcutta – Clive restored British rule and went on to defeat the Bengalis at the Battle of Plassey.

Coming home again, Clive served as MP for Shrewsbury before another spell in India. But by now there were enemies, and accusations of treachery and dishonesty. It was obvious that he was also manic depressive. Robert Clive died in mysterious circumstances at his home in London, and was buried in an unmarked grave in the churchyard at Moreton Say.

Places to Visit

Tourist Information Centres

Oswestry ☎ 01691 662753

Ellesmere ☎ 01691 622981

Whitchurch ☎ 01948 664577

Market Drayton ☎ 01630 653114

Places of Interest

Oswestry

Park Hall Farm

Open in Summer, every day; Sept to Dec, Fri, Sat and Sun; Jan to Mar, Sat and Sun only. 10am–5pm
☎ 01691 671123
www.parkhallfarm.co.uk

Cambrian Railway Museum

Generally open from 1–5pm every day, but as staffing is voluntary, it is advisable to call first.
☎ 01691 671749
www.cambrianrailwayssociety.co.uk/Museum/museum

Whittington Castle

Free entry to castle grounds at any time (small parking fee). Tearoom open Mar to Oct Wed to Sun 10am–4pm, Nov to Feb Fri to Sun 10am–4pm

Ellesmere

The Meres Visitor Centre

Open Jul and Aug 11.30am–4.30pm; Apr to Jun, Sept, Oct 11am–4pm; Mar, Thur–Sun 11am–4pm; Nov and Dec weekends only 11am–4pm; closed Jan and Feb.
☎ 01691 622981

Whitchurch

Heritage Centre

Open Mon to Thur 9am–5pm, Friday 9am–4.30pm, Sat 10am–5pm, Sun closed.
☎ 01948 664577

Wem

Mythstories Museum

Open Apr to Aug 2.30pm–6.30pm (last admission 5.30pm) every day, Sept to Nov 11am–4pm (last admission 3pm) weekends only).
☎ 01939 235500
www.mythstories.com

Hawkstone Park Follies

Open all year except Nov and Dec (Santa's grotto only in Dec). Opening hours are complicated and best obtained from the website, but basically Winter opening is weekend only; Spring and Autumn, Wed to Sun; Summer and all school holidays, every day. Gates always open at 10am, and last admission times vary from 2.30pm–4pm.
☎ 01939 200611
www.hawkstone.co.uk

Hodnet Hall Gardens

Open special days only 12noon to 5pm. Groups at other times by appointment. Details can best be obtained by telephone or from the website.
☎ 01630 685786
www.hodnethallgardens.org

Wollerton Old Hall Gardens

Open Fri, Sun and Bank Holidays from Good Fri to the end of Sept 12noon–5pm.
☎ 01630 685760
www.wollertonoldhallgarden.com

Best Walks

* Ellesmere offers a good town map showing local walks. A short circuit of 1½ miles incorporates canal, Mere and castle mound, and can be extended to a 7-mile circuit through Welshampton. All Ellesmere's routes are marked with a flying swan logo – very helpful!

* In this fairly flat countryside, there are few good viewpoints. Hen Dinas near Oswestry gives one of the widest perspectives, but Grinshill is in a class of its own

* The canal towpath. For maximum boating interest, walk from Whitchurch down to Grindley Brook locks; for maximum drama, cross Chirk aqueduct (and go on into Darkie Tunnel); for maximum vegetation (and possibly mud), walk from Market Drayton through Woodseaves Cutting.

* Finally the Offa's Dyke Path. 180 miles is a big undertaking but you could whet your appetite for the whole by walking just the particularly attractive stretch north of Llanymynech. Bus connections are poor so you may need a taxi for out or return journeys.

On your bike

• North Shropshire District Council has produced four excellent free leaflets of circular Cycle Rides – 5 routes around Ellesmere, 5 routes around Wem, 4 around Whitchurch and 4 around Market Drayton. Maps and directions are very clear, snippets of local interest are offered, and for the most part the routes follow minor roads. Obtainable from any Tourist Office in the area.

• Three other leaflets relate to the National Cycle network co-ordinated by the charity Sustrans. Look out for information on Route 31 (Oswestry – Whitchurch), Route 45 (Whitchurch – Shrewsbury) and Route 81 (Welshpool – Shrewsbury)

For the family

* Park Hall offers simple unsophisticated entertainment for young families (bouncy castles, pedal tractors, sand-pits, cart rides, etc.) along with the opportunity to meet farm animals and pets. Attached tearoom-cum-café fulfils all food requirements.

* Hawkstone Park Follies. This bizarre world appeals to all ages (although the most exciting paths are not really suitable for pushchairs). Choose a fine day and bring a torch and a picnic.

* Hire a day boat on the canal. Not inexpensive, but enormous fun! Day boats usually have outdoor covered seating, and an enclosed galley area where it is possible to at least make a cup of tea. Young children need to be watched like a hawk (and older ones perhaps even more so!) but you can expect life jackets to be provided. Day boats are available from marinas marked on Page 14.

A rainy day

* Park Hall Farm again. With the exception of the picnic woodland, everything is under cover. It can be cold in winter, though!

* Mythstories at Wem. They guarantee to tell you at least one story, but you could spend a long time listening to others on disc (and video)

* Enjoy lunch at the Boathouse at Ellesmere where you can watch the raindrops falling on the Mere.

23

2. Shrewsbury & around

High the vanes of Shrewsbury gleam
Islanded in Severn stream

Housman's few words beautifully portray the unique situation of Shropshire's county town. Shrewsbury sits on a hill tightly cradled in a deep loop of the River Severn. Over the centuries the river has effectively acted as its moat, with the gap between the ends of the loop – a mere 300 yards or so – defended by the addition of a castle in the 11th century.

Today the town inside that coil of river is largely Tudor, the hilltop spires of St Mary's and St Alkmund's looking down on a lattice of narrow streets and alleyways with curious names like Dogpole, Wyle Cop, Grope Lane and Mardol. Half-timbered 'magpie' buildings are plentiful, but there is also a fine stone 16th century market hall, a medieval abbey, the remains of a Norman castle and a lot more. The 20th century has crept in of course – whoever thought the brick tower of the Indoor Market Hall would enhance the scene? But all in all, Shrewsbury boasts something like 660 listed buildings – and surrounding them, the lawns and lime avenues of Quarry Park provide a pleasant skirt of green along the banks of the encircling river. More colour is added to the scene by Shrewsbury's award-winning floral displays and by a summer season that includes events like Street Theatre and Morris Dancing. In mid-August, the renowned Shrewsbury Flower Show attracts around 75,000 visitors, who enjoy not only the blooms but regional produce, music, entertainment and the hundreds of fascinating stalls set out in Quarry Park.

Shrewsbury, also famed as the birthplace of Charles Darwin, has more than enough to offer all its visitors, but there is more of interest in the countryside around. To the north, the story of the Battle of Shrewsbury (1403) is told on the ground where it was fought. Walks are laid out around the fields here – and there are more easy rambles to be had on sandstone Nesscliffe Hill and farther south at Lyth Hill Country Park. The 13th century fortified manor house at Acton Burnell, Attingham Park with its extensive grounds and Regency interior, the haunting silhouette of Haugh-

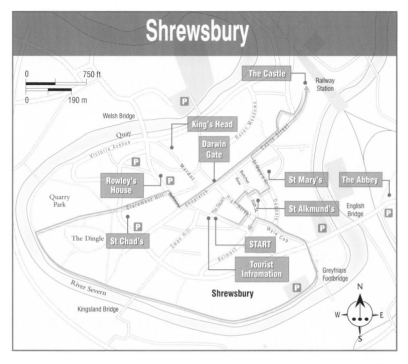

Shrewsbury

0	750 ft
0	190 m

The Castle
Railway Station

Welsh Bridge

King's Head

Quay

Darwin Gate

Victoria Avenue

Mardol

Raven Meadows

Castle Street

Butcher Row

Rowley's House

Quarry Park

Claremont Hill

Shoplatch

Pride Hill

St Mary's

The Abbey

St Alkmund's

English Bridge

The Dingle

St Chad's

Swan Hill

The Square

High Street

Wyle Cop

Dogpole

Belmont

START

Tourist Infromation

Greyfriars Footbridge

Shrewsbury

River Severn

Kingsland Bridge

N
W — E
S

mond Abbey and the well-preserved Roman site of Wroxeter are just a few more attractions in the vicinity.

Shrewsbury

Shrewsbury's naturally defensive site led to its settlement by refugees from Wroxeter at the time the Romans were abandoning their town. These early inhabitants named their new abode Pengwern, or 'alder hill', while to the later Saxons it became Scrobbesbyrig. After the Norman conquest, the town (along with most of Shropshire) was given to William the Conqueror's favoured kinsman Roger de Montgomerie, and it was he who built the first castle to

In Grope Lane

breach the gap in the watery defences. He was also responsible for the building of the first abbey, a Benedictine establishment, on the site of a wooden church to the east of the town.

Roger's castle soon fell to King Stephen (1138) but later managed to hold out successfully against the repeated attacks of the Welsh. The abbey prospered, and from 1283 onwards was home to the meetings of Edward I's First English Parliament.

The 1403 Battle of Shrewsbury (see P.34) was fought beyond the confines of the town (to the north) and so caused no damage, but the later Civil War was a different story. Shrewsbury was a Royalist stronghold, and its castle was soon taken and wrecked by the Parliamentarians. The abbey suffered likewise when Royalist prisoners were held within its ancient walls. But Shrewsbury prospered on account of the wool trade and its streets were lined with the homes of wealthy merchants. Many of these fine buildings remain today, as do many of the medieval alleyways linking them, and although castle and abbey have undergone changes over the years, there is still plenty to see. As John Betjeman observed, 'It takes a little exploration on foot to reveal the delights of this medieval town'.

A stroll around the town

Whichever way you go, it is simply impossible to take in all there is to see in Shrewsbury in a few hours. The Tourist Office can offer a couple of themed routes and the website www.shrewsburyguide.info has yet another tour. The route described here is a blend of the most important places along with some snippets of the Darwin story, one or two of the best 'shuts' (medieval alleyways) and a stroll through the beautiful gardens and riverside park.

The best place to start any exploration of Shrewsbury is **The Square**, because it is right in the centre of town, and wherever you park the car, you will soon find it signed on one of the handsome wrought iron fingerposts (If you use the Park and Ride service, the bus will drop you nearby in High Street). At one end of The Square, a statue of Clive of India looks out across the High Street, while at the other end the stone-arched 16th century **Old Market Hall** rejoices in its recent restoration. On the opposite side of the road here, the Victorian **Music Hall** serves as both Theatre and Tourist Information Office (although the theatre will be moving in 2009), so this is the place to pick up any further information you might want on the town.

Standing with your back to the Music Hall, the street to your right is Princess Street, with the very popular Gallery Tea Rooms a hundred yards or so along on the right. Continuing past the tearooms, you will soon reach the Golden Cross Hotel on the opposite side, and just beyond it, **Golden Cross Passage**. This is definitely Shrewsbury's most attractive shut, flanked by bistros, and overlooked by the spire of St Alkmund's.

At the end of the shut, turn left on High Street and walk back towards the Square. Just before reaching it, look out for an old half-timbered building on the opposite side of the road. Some of its timbers and carvings have recently been restored and it is said that the new versions include effigies of Margaret Thatcher and Mick Jagger (do they?).

The building is actually on the corner of a narrow alleyway called **Grope Lane**. Continue up Grope Lane into **Fish Street**, the much photographed medieval heart of the town. To the right the old Three Fishes Inn crouches under the shadow of St Alkmund's, while to the left the cobbled street curves round into picturesque Butcher Row.

Diagonally across Fish Street, **Bear Steps** pass under a half-timbered

Half-timbered houses

In the Middle Ages, Shropshire oak was widely used in construction work. In the countryside, houses were often simply 'cruck-framed', the cruck being two curved beams of wood set apart at the base and united at the apex. The framework was used for both walls and roofs, and was then generally filled in with other material so that there was no external evidence of the timber frame. Box-framed houses were very much more robust and more often found in towns. Vertical, horizontal and even diagonal beams were used, with certain beams being structures of major support. The houses were built on a layer of local red sandstone and usually topped with a roof of Welsh slate. Since this was heavy, the sturdiness of the supporting framework was essential, and has contributed to the survival of so many of these houses to this day. Shrewsbury has a particular wealth of box-framed houses, but you will find plenty more throughout the county – and indeed all over the West Midlands.

building that is now an art gallery and café. Go up the steps to emerge in St Alkmund's Place, a shady spot to sit and perhaps enjoy a coffee at one of the outdoor tables. The spire of **St Alkmund's Church** peers down from a grand height of 184ft, and the church itself is most renowned for its east window dating from 1795, in which the main figure is a copy of Reni's *Assumption of the Virgin*. Splendid as this window is, it is merely an aperitif for what lies around the corner!

Walk around St Alkmund's Place to leave it on Church Street, dominated by the bar of Shrewsbury's oldest hotel, the Prince Rupert (a nephew of Charles I, he once lived here). Emerging on **St Mary's** Street, the church of that name is directly opposite. This fine church has one of the highest spires in England, but its crowning glory is its magnificent stained glass, said to be the best collection of such in the country. Seemingly none of it was originally made for the church! Best of all is the Jesse window filling the east end, a depiction of the man himself with the vine growing from his loins winding through ranks of richly-coloured kings and prophets to reach Mary and Joseph in the tracery above. The window dates from the first half of the 14th century and is thought to have been made for the Franciscan church in Shrewsbury before being installed in St Chad's and then moved to St Mary's. More remarkable glass can be seen in the centre of the north wall. This relates to the life of St. Bernard of Clairvaux, and was made for the Abbey of Altenburg near Cologne around 1550, and bought for St Mary's in the early 19th century. The glass is now so prized that in 2007 each panel was carefully taken down and returned to Germany for exhibition, St Mary's making do with perspex copies during its absence. Other glass at St Mary's comes from Trier, from the Netherlands and from Belgium, all of it very old, and all a feast for the eyes. The carvings in the splendid oak ceiling are also worthy of inspection.

When you can tear yourself away from the glories of St Mary's, continue up St Mary's Street, finally turning right on Castle Street to reach **Shrewsbury Castle**. The gateway here is the only feature remaining of the original 11th century building. Restored and rebuilt by Edward I, it was further altered over the years and finally fell into disrepair after it was captured by the Parliamentarians in the Civil War. The castle you see today has had the hand of Thomas Telford laid upon it – in 1787 he was invited to convert the derelict building into a home for the town's MP Sir William Pulteney. Across the manicured lawns and immaculate flower beds, Laura's Tower is a folly that was added for his wife. The castle itself houses a three-floor museum crammed with memorabilia of the Shropshire Regiment.

Across the road from the castle, the grey-stoned Library building was once

Fish Street

The square and Market Hall

Shrewsbury School, and a statue of its most famous pupil looks solemnly down from its plinth before the entrance. Charles Darwin, biologist and author of the momentous *On the Origin of Species* was born in Shrewsbury in 1809, and became a boarder at the school.

From the statue, bear left up the cobbled road to meet Castle Street again. Turn right here, and walk through the pedestrianised shopping area of Pride Hill until you reach the new glass and copper sculpture at Darwin Gate. To the right here, Mardol runs down to the river. It is an old street with many interesting houses, but most worthy of a diversion is the **King's Head Inn**, on the right at the bottom. Dating from the 15th century its upper stories bulge over the road, while recent interior restoration has revealed a painting of the Last Supper on the chimney breast in the bar (on the right as you enter).

Back again at Darwin Gate, continue ahead up Shoplatch, passing the new Market Hall to take the first road on the right, Bellstone. Walking under the arch into the courtyard of the Morris Hall, you will find a huge glacial boulder known as the **Bellstone** proudly displayed. The stone is reputed to have been 'the young Charles Darwin's introduction to geology'.

After passing the Bellstone Hotel, the road ahead is Barker Street, with handsome black-and-white **Rowley's House** (now the town museum and art gallery) sadly stranded between car parks. A minute's walk will take you down to it, but this circular journey continues by turning left after the Bellstone Hotel to climb Claremont Hill. Among these fine Georgian houses, no. 13 was the home of the Unitarian minister who gave Darwin his early education. At the top of the hill stands the church where Darwin was baptised. **St Chad's** was built in 1792 and displays the classic Greek features fashionable at the time. Its more recently acquired point of interest is a gravestone with the name Ebenezer Scrooge, tucked among others in the churchyard! You may recognise it (and St Chad's) from the 1984 film *A Christmas Carol*.

From St Chad's, cross the road and take the path across the sloping green lawns of **Quarry Park** to the river. On the left of this path is The Dingle, a sunken floral garden with lake and fountains. A bust of Percy Thrower reminds you that for 28 years the cel-

St Alkmund's Place

ebrated television horticulturalist was head gardener in Shrewsbury – The Dingle was his creation.

Reaching the statue of Hercules on the riverside, the path to the right leads round to Welsh Bridge and beside it, flower-bedecked **Victoria Quay**, the starting point for boat trips on the river. Leave that for later and instead turn left, walking under avenues of limes with present-day Shrewsbury School looking down from its perch high on the far bank. The more elegant of the two boathouses belongs to the school. Pass under the first bridge (although it offers a quick return to town) and continue to the next crossing, Greyfriars Footbridge. Turn left here and a lane will take you up to a road junction at the foot of Wyle Cop.

Wyle Cop has many fine 'magpie' buildings – and one or two interesting shuts as well – and it will take you straight back to the top of the town, High Street and The Square. But at this point you are quite close to **Shrewsbury Abbey** – it stands about 400 yards away, across English Bridge to the right. If you prefer not to divert on foot but to go by car later, there is a car park opposite. The abbey church is all that

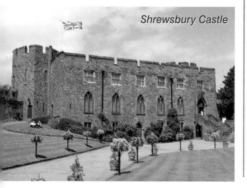
Shrewsbury Castle

29

Charles Darwin (1809-1882)

Charles Darwin was the fifth child of a wealthy Shrewsbury physician, and was born at The Mount on the west side of the town. After first attending a Unitarian school he went on to board at Anglican Shrewsbury School. At the age of 16 he left to study medicine at Edinburgh, but finding it not to his taste, soon transferred to Cambridge to read theology. Once again he found distractions in the form of natural history and geology, but at the same time earned himself a good degree. Having no real desire to enter the church, he obtained the post of gentleman's companion to Robert Fitzroy, the captain of HMS Beagle. The ship was setting out to chart the coastline of South America, but in practice it spent five years in the seas of the southern hemisphere, with Darwin collecting fossils and observing living organisms at every stop. On his return Darwin soon became a celebrity in the scientific world, and from his notes, The Voyage of HMS Beagle was published in 1839.

Already Darwin was forming ideas of natural selection, and of known life forms having one or more common ancestors, but he diverted to study barnacles for eight years before publishing On the Origin of Species by Means of Natural Selection in 1859. It was a best seller! Darwin had been careful not to bring man into his evolutionary arguments, but the implications were obviously there and it was not long before the church reacted against it and heated debates ensued. Darwin kept himself in the background, and although adding fuel to the fire with his subsequent publication The Descent of Man, decided to devote the rest of his life to botanical studies.

Perceived to be a great man in his own lifetime, Charles Darwin was accorded a state funeral and was buried in Westminster Abbey alongside Herschel and Newton. His latter-day home, Down House in Kent, has been preserved as a museum and is now in the care of English Heritage. Shrewsbury celebrates its greatest son with a Darwin Festival, held in February each year.

remains of the large complex that was here before the Dissolution and before Telford drove his Holyhead Road this way – or almost all, because an isolated refectory pulpit stands across the road. The red sandstone church looks a little sorry for itself stranded on a triangle of green beside a busy main road, but Shrewsbury Abbey has found many latter-day admirers on account of its role in the Brother Cadfael novels.

Fiction aside, the abbey is a solid Norman building in which many original features remain. Inside, huge pillars support high rounded arches and among the effigies on the tombstones is a battered one of its founder Roger de Montgomerie, who died in 1094. Sadly there can be no reminder of the abbey's important role when from 1283 onwards, Edward I's First English Parliament held meetings in the long-vanished chapter house. A recent addition to the grounds is a modern memorial to the war poet Wilfred Owen.

Percy Thrower (1913-1988)

Percy Thrower was the very first television gardener and his bust in the Dingle recognises that it was this particular piece of garden that set him on the road to fame. Percy had worked in several places (including the Royal Gardens at Windsor) before being appointed head gardener at Shrewsbury in 1945. In this role, one of his first projects was the restoration of the Dingle, which had been sadly neglected over the war years. Visiting Quarry Park some two years later, radio presenter Godfrey Baseley was so impressed that he asked to meet its creator - and invited him on to his show, 'Beyond the Back Door'. Percy's warmth and ease of communication ensured his success, and he later moved from radio to television, becoming associated with Country Calendar, Out and About, Gardeners' World and finally Blue Peter.

Over the years Percy Thrower also wrote regular columns for several daily papers, articles for the magazine Amateur Gardening and many books, including his memoirs My Lifetime of Gardening. He was awarded the MBE in 1984. In Shrewsbury he was instrumental in establishing the very successful Flower Show, and opened the Percy Thrower Gardening Centre (near Meole Brace, south of the town), which is still run by his three daughters.

Brother Cadfael

Brother Cadfael of Shrewsbury Abbey, 12th century monk-cum-detective, was the inspired creation of Shropshire writer Edith Pargeter, writing under the pseudonym Ellis Peters. She had many other novels to her name (and being a self-taught Czech speaker, had also translated many books from that language), but it is for her 20 stories of the unusually-worldly, mischievous, sympathetic herbalist monk that she will be remembered. After a series of radio adaptations, Central Television broadcast 13 of the stories as feature-length dramas (1994-1998), with Sir Derek Jacobi playing the part of Brother Cadfael.

Around Shrewsbury

4 miles south-west of Shrewsbury (off the Ironbridge road) lies the old Roman town of Viroconium, now usually known by the name of the nearby village, **Wroxeter**. Originally just a military camp beside busy Watling Street, it grew and developed, until by the 2nd century AD it was the fourth largest town in Britain (after London, St Albans and Cirencester), and the capital of the Cornovii region. The walls, more than two miles in length, enclosed an area of 600 acres in which around 6000 people were living affluent and civilised lives. Most of this area has never been excavated and today sheep graze over the humps and hollows that hold their secrets. Nevertheless, English Heritage has taken into its care the civic centre of the town, comprising an administrative

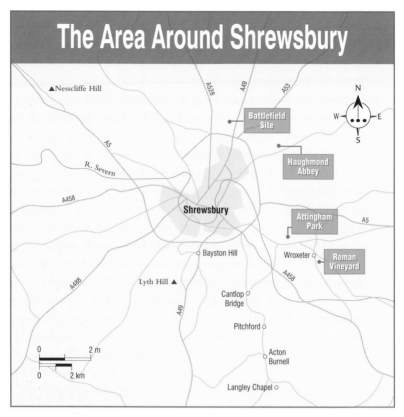

The Area Around Shrewsbury

▲Nesscliffe Hill

A528

A49

A53

Battlefield Site

N
W — E
S

A5

R. Severn

Haughmond Abbey

A458

Shrewsbury

Attingham Park

A5

Bayston Hill

Wroxeter ○

Roman Vineyard

A488

Lyth Hill ▲

Cantlop ○
Bridge

A458

A49

Pitchford ○

0   2 m
0   2 km

Acton ○
Burnell

Langley Chapel ○

Rowley's House

Attingham Park

basilica alongside the public bath house. Between them stand the 'Old Work', one of the largest preserved sections of Roman wall in the country. Also identifiable are the various rooms of the bath house, part of the furnace that once heated the water, and the separating colonnades.

Beside the site there is now a Visitor Centre with explanations of Roman life at the time, and a few of the finds on display. Other artefacts have been taken to the town museum in Shrewsbury. Viroconium was abandoned early in the 6th century, but it is known that a local chieftain – possibly even King Arthur – later made his capital in the ruined city.

The Romans certainly grew vines to produce their wine at Wroxeter, and just down the road (through the village), the vines of the new **Wroxeter Roman Vineyard** were planted in 1991. They were carefully chosen to be suitable for this most northerly site. Today Wroxeter produces red, white and rosé wines, all given appropriate names like Roman Villa, Noble Roman and Wrekin Reserve. The grapes are picked by hand and the wine is produced on the site. You are welcome to wander through the vineyard and watch whatever work is in progress – and of course, to taste and purchase the wines!

Darwin in front of the old Shrewsbury School

St Chad's

The Battle of Shrewsbury (July 21st, 1403)

The events of the Battle of Shrewsbury are perhaps best known as the climax to Shakespeare's play Henry IV Part I. The background to the story is that in 1399 Henry IV had deposed his rival Richard II, but then failed to honour his promises of land and money to those who had supported him. Henry 'Hotspur' Percy of Northumberland and his uncle Thomas Percy of Worcester felt particularly wronged, and set about raising a rebel army. Henry met them near Shrewsbury, offered terms which were rejected, and a 3-hour battle ensued. Hotspur and something like 2,000 soldiers of both sides were killed in that short time, before the rebel army fled in disarray. The dead were buried on the battlefield, and the Church of St Mary Magdalene was later built as a memorial over their grave.

Just to the north of Wroxeter, alongside the B4380, stands **Attingham Park**, one of the greatest country houses in Shropshire. Set in 500 acres of parkland, it was built of Grinshill sandstone in 1785 to the designs of George Steuart, with later alterations being made by John Nash. Having passed through the hands of eight generations of the Berwick family, it is now in the care of the National Trust, and is still undergoing restoration. Visits include the main dining room with its sumptuous plasterwork and marble fireplace, the 'trompe d'oeil' drawing room, the romantic ladies' boudoir, the Nash picture gallery and the kitchen and servants quarters – and there are fine collections of Regency furniture and silverware. Outside, the parkland is equally delightful, with marked walks laid out through rhododendron woodland, around the Deerpark and along the banks of the River Tern. Children are well-catered for at Attingham with a play area in the grounds and activity packs and quizzes in the house. Holiday times bring added activities such as an Easter Egg Hunt or a Letter-Box Trail.

An outpost of Attingham is Cronkhill, Nash's first Italianate villa, half a mile way on the road south beside the Severn. Cronkhill is currently open just 6 days a year.

In the grounds of **Attingham Park** (near the entrance), Attingham Home Farm is another venue perfect for families. Everyone can enjoy watching the daily activities like milking on this traditional working farm, and there are added special events in the school holidays. The farm houses some rare breeds of cattle, sheep, pigs and fowl.

In the off-the-beaten track country to the south of Attingham, a string of interesting places lie along the same minor road. From Shrewsbury or from its by-pass, take the A458 Bridgnorth road, and then turn right (SP Acton Burnell Castle, Cantlop Bridge) immediately south of the by-pass. The same little road can be reached from Attingham by heading south through Cross Houses and Berrington.

The first brief pause on this road is **Cantlop Bridge**, about 3 miles from the by-pass. A single span cast iron bridge, it was built by Thomas Telford in 1813 to carry the road across Cound

Brook. No longer in use, it stands resplendent beside today's road with a pull-in for visitors and a display board explaining some of its technicalities.

Continuing south from Cantlop, the road runs through **Pitchford**, and well before the village, you will see a signed turn to Pitchford Church. The originally Norman sandstone building stands in a delightful setting among old yew trees beyond an avenue of limes. There is no right of access past the church, but from the churchyard you can glimpse the north side of Pitchford Hall, said by Pevsner to be 'the most splendid piece of black-and-white building in Shropshire'. The better view is probably from the south side where there are projecting wings, but the dazzling geometric patterns and curious star-shaped chimneys are still impressive. Pitchford was built around 1560, provided a hiding place for Prince Rupert after the Civil war siege of Shrewsbury, and naturally has several resident ghosts. A Grade I listed building it is sadly unoccupied and in need of repair.

Through Pitchford the road reaches the village of **Acton Burnell**. Signs direct you to the 'Castle', which in fact is a ruined 13th century fortified manor house, originally the home of one Robert Burnell, Chancellor of England and close friend of Edward I. Its finest hour came when Edward I summoned his very first English Parliament (Commons as well as Lords) to meet in a barn here in 1283 (it later met at Shrewsbury Abbey). Later falling to ruin, the castle became a folly in the grounds of 18th century Acton Hall. Today the Hall is used as a private college and the castle is cared for by English Heritage. Overhung by the spreading blue branches of an aged Cedar, its red sandstone walls and towers surely form Shropshire's most handsome ruin.

A mile or so beyond Acton Burnell a left turn leads on to **Langley Chapel**, the last of the 'sights' on this road. A simple building with a low weatherboard belfry, it stands isolated in a roadside field. The remarkable feature at Langley is the furnishings, which as the building was abandoned less than a century after it was built, have remained as they were first installed. Whitewashed walls, pulpit, reading desk, high box pews, rough-hewn seats and table rather than altar bear witness to early 17th century Puritan worship. Again English Heritage cares for the site, and the door is regularly left open.

Back again at Attingham and the signed road to the north will take you to **Haughmond Abbey**. Records reveal that the abbey on this gentle hillside was in existence early in the 12th century, when it was a humble Augustinian establishment. Its heyday came half a century on, when it attracted the patronage of the wealthy FitzAlan family of Clun, who were friends of Henry II. The FitzAlans tombs can be seen in the remains of the abbey church. The abbey was abandoned at the Dissolution (1539), and its buildings were later used as a working farm. Today it is under the care of English Heritage. Parts of the abbots' quarters and refectory remain, but most impressive is the chapter house, with its intricate carvings of saints within the arches (those martyred stand on the heads of their oppressors, as in John the Baptist and King Herod).

More carvings of St Peter and St Paul can be found in the remaining part of the cloister.

The abbey looks down over the flat country to the north of Shrewsbury, and here it was that the **Battle of Shrewsbury** was fought in 1403. The monks must have had the best view of that particularly bloody encounter. The positions taken up by the King (Henry IV) and the rebel army are not precisely known, but a gravel track has been laid around the fields where it was fought, starting from a viewpoint off the Whitchurch road. The route includes St Mary Magdalene Church and Battlefield Farm, whose outbuildings house a small exhibition (and also a very well-stocked organic shop and an excellent tearoom)

The battlefield site offers a good walk in its own right, and farther to the west, **Nesscliffe Hill** (off the A5), is another interesting scene to be explored on foot. Pines and rhododendrons clothe this sandstone outcrop and there are fine views of the not-too-far-away Breidden Hills from its summit. Near the east end of the hill (take the access track nearest to the road through the village) is Kynaston's Cave, a huge recess in a sheer

Mary Webb (1881-1927)

The oldest daughter of a schoolteacher, Mary Gladys Meredith was born in Leighton (8 miles south-east of Shrewsbury) and spent almost all her life in Shropshire, which she loved. Although writing poetry and short stories from an early age, she began to do so more prolifically after her marriage to Henry Webb in 1912. The Golden Arrow was published in 1916, Gone to Earth the next year and several others followed. All were imbued with a strong sense of Shropshire, its countryside and its people. Mary Webb suffered all her life with the disfiguring thyroid disorder Graves' Disease (she herself was the role model for the hare-lipped Prue Sarn in Precious Bane) and died at the age of 46. Her talents were never seriously recognised in her time, acclaim coming only after 1928 when Prime Minister Stanley Baldwin addressed the Literary Fund dinner and described her as a 'neglected genius'. Gone to Earth was filmed in 1950 and Precious Bane shown as a television play in 1989. Shrewsbury Tourist Office should be able to find you a leaflet of four trails (The Magic of Shropshire with Mary Webb) visiting sites that were important in the life of Mary Webb, or in her novels.

Victoria Quay, Shrewsbury

sandstone cliff that in the 16th century was home to the local 'Robin Hood' highwayman, Humphrey Kynaston. The worn steps that were his only access are closed off today, but if you could climb them, you would see two rooms, one for Humphrey and one for his horse, with the initials H.K. engraved on the partition between them. Humphrey

Haughmond Abbey

St Mary's Church with Jesse window

Battlefield Church

escaped the law here for several years, aided and abetted by the local poor who benefited from his spoils, and died in the cave in 1534.

To the south of Nesscliffe (off the A49 south of Shrewsbury), **Lyth Hill** Country Park is a very different spot for an upland ramble. Although only a mere 169m in height, its stretches of open grassland and scattered coppice offer a magnificent prospect of the Shropshire horizon. A toposcope identifies every detail. The hill and its view were much beloved by novelist Mary Webb, who for the last ten years of her life lived close to the summit in the cottage she had designed (Spring Cottage, now extended and privately owned).

Wroxeter Roman Baths

Shrewsbury Flower Show

Places to Visit

Tourist Information Centres

Shrewsbury ☎ 01743 281200

Places of Interest

Shrewsbury Castle and Shropshire Regimental Museum

There is free access to the castle grounds Mon to Sat 9am–5pm, and also Sun between late May and mid-Sept.
Museum open late May to mid-Sept daily, 10am–5pm (4pm Sun); mid-Feb to late May, Tue to Sat 10am–4pm.
☎ 01743 358516

Shrewsbury Museum and Art Gallery (Rowley's House)

Open late May to mid-Sept, daily 10am–5pm (4pm Sun); late Mar to late May, Tue to Sat 10am–4pm.
☎ 01743 361196

Wroxeter Roman City

Open Mar to Oct 10am–5pm daily; Nov to Feb 10am–4pm Wed to Sun.
☎ 01743 761330

Wroxeter Roman Vineyard

Open Mon to Sat 11am–5pm, Sun 12noon–5.30pm.
☎ 01743 761888

Attingham Park

Park, shop and reception open daily, 9am–6pm mid-Feb to Oct; Nov to mid-Feb 9am–5pm.
House open mid-Mar to Oct 1–5.30pm daily except Wed. Guided tours between 11an and 1pm when house is open.
☎ 01743 708123

Cronkhill

Dates and times of opening can be obtained by phoning ☎ 01743 708123 (Attingham Park)

Attingham Home Farm

Open late Mar to Sept daily except Fridays, 12noon–5,30pm (school holidays daily 11am–5.30pm); Oct to Dec weekends only 12noon–5pm (Oct half-term daily 11am–5pm).
☎ 01743 709243

Acton Burnell Castle

Free access 'at any reasonable time'

Langley Chapel

Free access daily, Mar to Oct 10am–5pm; Nov to Feb 10am–4pm

Haughmond Abbey

Open late Mar to Sept 10am–5pm Wed to Sun and Bank Holidays.
☎ 01743 709661

Take a Walk

* The riverside in Shrewsbury is excellent for a short stroll – and if you fancy extending it, remember that the waymarked Severn Way follows the river all the way from its source on Plynlimon to the sea at Gloucester!

* The route around the Battlefield site is an easy 1½ mile walk on a gravelled path suitable for pushchairs and wheelchairs (there is just one slight incline). The bonus is the possibility of en route refreshment at Battlefield Farm.

* The dense woods of Nesscliffe and open grassland of Lyth Hill offer contrasting upland rambles (with views)

On your bike

* Shrewsbury already has 20 miles of dedicated cycle route and more than 200 places to park a bike. In June 2008 it won its bid to become one of 11 new 'cycling towns', so over the next three years will be extending and improving these facilities, and offering more information and training.

* If you have young children with you, you may like to get hold of Shropshire's Family Cycling Guide, which offers (among others), a Scenic Shrewsbury Ride of 10 or 20 miles, much of it off road. The guide is available from any Tourist Information or can be downloaded from www.shropshirecycling.co.uk

* National Cycle Route 81 heads west from Shrewsbury (Quarry Park) to Wellington, a distance of 13 miles on country lanes with not too demanding gradients.

For the Family

* Quarry Park has lots of grassland for ball games and a children's play area at the Victoria Quay end.

* Attingham Park and its Home Farm between them offer at least a whole day's family entertainment. See the text.

* Taking a walk never seems to appeal to young children but there is plenty of play potential in the woodland of Nesscliffe Hill, and you can at least get a glimpse of romantic Kynaston's Cave.

A rainy day

* As well as its many individual shops, Shrewsbury has 3 indoor shopping malls - the Darwin Centre, Pride Hill Centre and The Parade (with independent specialist shops). It may be an expensive way of passing the day!

* The Regimental Museum and Rowley's House should each keep you in the dry for an hour while you pore over their collections.

* Attingham again. Guided tours of the house take around an hour, but you can take all the time you want if you do it independently.

3. Blue Remembered Hills
– The South-west

What are those blue remembered hills
What spires, what farms are those?

This south-west corner of the county is home to the 'blue remembered hills' of Housman's epic. The poet was a native not of Shropshire but of Worcestershire, and these beautiful hills formed the western horizon of his childhood. Fifty years ago, the Shropshire Hills were designated an Area of Outstanding Natural Beauty.

Shropshire's uplands exist as a series of parallel ridges, each one running from north-east to south-west – the jagged quartzite peaks of the Stiperstones in the west are succeeded by the humpbacks of the Long Mynd, and then by the Stretton Hills. Farthest east is the long escarpment of Wenlock Edge, but outliers like the Clee Hills and the Wrekin are also included in the protected area. The Shropshire Hills are a walker's paradise with everything from gentle valley strolls to demanding high moorland hikes on offer. For those who visit by car, the scenery is outstanding, and timeless small towns like Bishop's

Left: Looking down Hope Dale

Left: Looking down Hope Dale

Opposite page: Townsbrook Hollow, Long Mynd

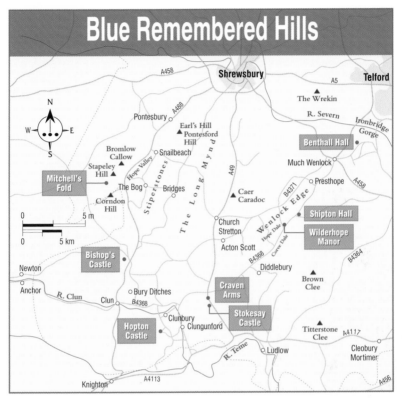

Blue Remembered Hills

Castle and Clun with their populations of artists and craftsmen provide added fascination. Church Stretton nestling under the Long Mynd beguiles with a faded Edwardian air, while Ludlow in the south was described by John Betjeman as 'probably the loveliest town in England'.

Into the Hills

The Hope Valley

Leaving Shrewsbury on the A488, it is only a few minutes before the twin cones of **Earl's Hill** and **Pontesford Hill** burst dramatically on to the horizon in the south. Earl's Hill was Shropshire Wildlife Trust's very first nature reserve back in 1964, and is renowned particularly for its plant life. The track to the summit is steep, but the panorama more than compensates for the effort! Farther on, beyond Pontesbury and Minsterley, the road enters **Hope Valley**, which has its own nature reserve (and splendid viewpoint) in the woodland alongside the road. To the left here the land is rising steeply to the unseen rugged peaks of the Stiperstones, while on the right

41

Bromlow Callow

One of the summits on the west side of the Hope Valley is very distinctive. It is best seen by looking backwards (north) after the valley opens out. Bromlow Callow, a prominent mound with a perfect skull cap of pine trees, has been the subject of many a painting and photograph. It is said that the pines were planted there some centuries ago, to guide drovers coming from the west.

are a motley collection of lesser summits linked by upland plateau.

As the Hope Valley eventually widens, two of the most interesting hills in Shropshire appear ahead. The long low ridge of **Stapeley Hill** is followed by high almost-flat-topped Corndon – and both were sites favoured by prehistoric man. To take a closer look, turn right where signed to Stone Circle (beside ruined mine workings) and when the road bends sharp left, drive ahead up the track to a small car park. A walk of two hundred yards or so from here brings you to **Mitchell's Fold**, a ring of 15 stones (although there were once more) dating from the Bronze Age, around 2000 – 1200 BC. It is thought that Mitchell's Fold would have been a ceremonial site or maybe even a trading post. Whatever its original purpose, the site is full of atmosphere, with the Devil's Chair on Stiperstones peeping from behind the flank of a hill on the one side, and on the other, the long valleys stretching far away into mid-Wales. From Mitchell's Fold, the grassy track leads on across the brow of the hill to reach another stone circle, known as Hoarstone, 2 miles away. The whole

hill is peppered with Neolithic cairns, and a rather more energetic extension to this route includes a holy well and a hill top fortress. The prehistoric sites and pathways across Stapeley Hill are described in a brochure (*Stapeley Hill Historic Trails*) obtainable from local Tourist Offices and from The Bog Visitor Centre (see below).

Beyond Stapeley Hill, distinctive **Corndon** is of volcanic origin, and rises to 513m, a good 100m above its neighbour. It too boasts many prehistoric cairns, and its southern slopes are known to have been the site of a Bronze Age axe-head factory. Corndon is steep, but can easily be climbed starting from the car park near Mitchell's Fold. Walk back to the road, continue ahead on the track in the same direction (there is a Bronze Age long barrow in the field on the left), then go through a signed gate on the left to access the obvious track up the hill. The grassy summit of Corndon Hill is actually in Powys, and it is a truly magnificent viewpoint. To the west, all the great Welsh ranges (Plynlimon, Cadair Idris, Arans, Arenigs, Berwyns) line the horizon, with the Shropshire Hills nearer to hand and the Black Mountains and Malverns away to the south

The Stiperstones area

To the east of the Hope Valley rise the Stiperstones – the ridge can be accessed from the A488 by leaving at Plox Green in the north or a taking a turning 4 miles south signed to Pennerley. Stiperstones is formed of old Precambrian rock, some 480 million years of age. Weathering by frost and ice has left the summit with huge projecting shards of quartzite – and as you might expect in

Celtic Shropshire, the outcrops have been endowed with evocative names that are the very stuff of legends. The Devil holds court from his Chair, ghosts and witches gather at Manstone Rock on the longest night of the year, and Saxon chief Wild Edric, opponent of the invading Normans, is imprisoned with his men in the lead mines beneath the hill. Legend has it that Wild Edric comes out only to defend England in her hour of need (he was seen in 1914 and in 1939), but meanwhile he and his men can be heard tapping...

If you begin this exploration of the Stiperstones area at its northern end (approaching from Plox Green), the first village you reach has the curious name of Snailbeach. **Snailbeach** was once the centre of this area's lead mining industry – and proved rather a long tradition of exploitation here when in 1796 a lead ingot imprinted with the name of the Roman Emperor Hadrian was brought to light! In the latter half of the 19th century more than half of Shropshire's lead came from this single mine, and it was said to have been one of the most productive in Europe. Other mines were to be found on this west flank of Stiperstones (Tankerville and Shelve), and the area was not the quiet peaceful place that it is today. In 1990 Shropshire County Council bought the land around Snaibeach mine, and since that time several of its buildings, including the headgear of the George's shaft, have been restored. The site is now managed by the Shropshire Mines Trust, and has been invested with information panels. Visitors are welcome to wander around freely at any time, while on certain days it is possible to take a short guided trip into the mine.

From Snailbeach a path ascends through the trees to the summit of Stiperstones, but the climb is steep at this end of the ridge. Instead continue south on the road to the village of Stiperstones, where the friendly inn serves meals and snacks at all hours to restore the hungry walker. South again past Tankerville and Pennerley and you reach a spot prosaically named The Bog. This too was the site of a mine, and the houses of its workforce were pulled down in 1972. All that remains is the schoolroom, and

Walking on Stiperstones

The uneven stony track that runs along the top of the Stiperstones ridge can be accessed from many points (Snailbeach, the village of Stiperstones, The Bog, etc.), but the ascent is definitely easiest from The Knolls car park. A broad grassy track runs uphill to reach it near Cranberry Rock, the last outcrop of the line. To the right here the track climbs gently to Manstone Rock, the highest point of Stiperstones and, at 536m, the second highest in Shropshire. Farther north is the massive outcrop known as the Devil's Chair (don't dare to sit on it or he will conjure up a thunderstorm immediately) and then humble Shepherd's Rock. From there paths descend to Stiperstones village, Snailbeach and Habberley. It is possible to return on tracks along the flank of the hill (get the leaflet from The Bog) or in summertime to catch the Hills Shuttle bus that serves the whole area.

that has recently been put to good use as **The Bog Visitor Centre**. Staffed by volunteers, it serves teas and home-made cakes that are quite possibly the very best in Shropshire (Corndon Coffee Cake is good, but the prize must go to Bog Bake!). Local books, maps and craftwork are for sale and there are often demonstrations of rural skills such as woodcarving.

Leaving The Bog, the road bends on around the end of the Stiperstones ridge to reach a car park for the National Nature Reserve (known as The Knolls), the easiest point from which to reach the summit.

Most of Shropshire's ranges can be seen from the summit of Stiperstones, but to the east the scene is closed off by the long rounded hump of the Long Mynd across the green Ratlinghope valley. From The Knolls the road goes on that way, dipping to the very pretty hamlet of **Bridges**, home to one of Shropshire's six Youth Hostels. South of Stiperstones – from The Bog, The Knolls or Bridges – the roads will lead you to Bishop's Castle.

Bishop's Castle

No more than a low wall remains of the castle that was built here by a Bishop of Hereford almost a thousand years ago, but on the steep hillside beneath,

Bromlow Callow

Manstone Rock

George's Shaft, Snailbeach Mine

Blacksmith's Shop, Snailbeach Mine

Mitchell's Fold

Colours at Bishop's Castle

a most attractive town has grown up. Fortunately some of its medieval buildings are better preserved than its castle, among them the half-timbered Elizabethan 'House on Crutches' at the top of the High Street, now home to a charming local museum. Other buildings in Bishop's Castle are remarkable for the colours in which they are painted – deep blues stand side-by-side with pale yellows and rich terracottas, and there are even those that are patterned and multicoloured. How does it all blend so well? You could even be forgiven for thinking that the people in Bishop's Castle are wearing brighter-than-usual clothes!

The steep High Street of Bishop's Castle is the perfect place for browsing. Among the traditional old-fashioned shops are craftsmen's premises and rooms crammed with antiques. At the top of the town, the poppy-red second-hand bookshop doubles as a café (selling jewellery on the side) and not far away sounds of humming and ticking emerge from the dark recesses of well-stocked 'Clocks 'n Pots'. Farther down the street, there is hand-crafted furniture that is of such quality that it is only made to order – and the quaint premises of a little railway museum are proudly supported by a beam from an oak felled in the 14th century. A couple of stylish (and

delicately tinted) bistros in the vicinity may lure you to stay longer. A fascinating town today, Bishop's Castle grew up as an overnight halt for drovers from the Welsh hills on their way to the markets of London. Their route, known as the **Kerry Ridgeway**, can still be followed for 15 miles west to Cider House in Powys – and the many pubs of Bishop's Castle are a legacy of that time.

To the east of Stiperstones, the next range of hills is the Long Mynd. Its westerly face (the one visible from Stiperstones) is smooth and rounded, while the east side of the ridge is punctuated with deep branching valleys. It is this east flank that has most appeal for walkers and other visitors, and it is best accessed from the A49 running south from Shrewsbury. On this road, the first place of note is Church Stretton, and it is one of only two towns actually within the confines of the Area of Outstanding Natural Beauty.

Church Stretton

Church Stretton sits astride a deep valley, with the undulating peaks of the Stretton Hills on the east and the rounded back of the Long Mynd dominating on the opposite side. Although an ancient settlement, it rose to prominence in Victorian and Edwardian times

Museum of Local Life, Bishop's Castle

One-handed Clock, Bishop's Castle

Telling the Time

One curious feature at the lower end of the High Street in Bishop's Castle is the clock on the church tower, which has only one hand! It really isn't broken - it simply dates from an age when people's lives had no need of precise time, and an hour hand sufficed.

when 'spa water' was extracted from a glacial lake deep under the Long Mynd, and the town acquired the epithet 'Little Switzerland'. Today Church Stretton still has a turn-of-the-century feel, and one or two hotels persist with quiet references to the beneficial effects of the water. An Antiques emporium occupies a large slot in the centre of town, and the streets and alleyways around abound with interesting individual shops and tearooms. Older than all the other buildings is the Church of St Lawrence, mostly dating from Norman times. Tourist brochures mention only its Sheila-na-gig, a 'rude' pagan fertility symbol (see P.64) ensconced above the north doorway – but while there you might also cast a glance at the fine stained glass, 13th century heavy rafters and the latter-day collages that now brighten the dim interior.

From the town, it is easy to follow the brown signs to National Trust owned Carding Mill Valley, the easiest place from which to start exploring the Long Mynd.

The Long Mynd

The Long Mynd derives its title from the Welsh *mynydd* (mountain), and fits the name well, being a high ridge approximately 7 miles in length and barely 3 miles wide. Its moorland summit plateau rises only very gently to a highest point of 516m at Pole Bank, while the valleys (known as batches or hollows) on its eastern flank offer wild terrain for ramblers. These valleys are equally fascinating to geologists, because the old Precambrian rock that has been bent upwards in more recent upheavals now lies exposed on the surface in strata that in places are near-vertical. The summit plateau is particularly interesting for the Bronze Age dykes and trackways that cross it, and for its many ancient burial chambers.

Since 1965 much of the Long Mynd has been in the care of the National Trust, and in the **Carding Mill Valley** they have provided car parking and a Chalet Pavilion serving light meals and home bakery. In the adjacent gift shop you can pick up leaflets and maps that will guide you on to the mountain.

Church Stretton's valley is actually on the line of a geological fault, and the town has experienced several earthquakes – although none too serious! The east side of the Stretton valley is formed by the volcanic **Stretton Hills**, a line of summits of which the highest and most obvious is **Caer Caradoc**. Its rocky peak is crowned by an Iron Age hill fort said to have been the scene of the last battle between the ancient Briton chief Caractacus (Caradoc in Welsh) and the invading Romans – although it must be said that other sites in Britain claim the same distinction. From Church

Stretton there are good walks over Caer Caradoc and the hills on either side (The Lawley in the north and Ragleth in the south).

Craven Arms

South of Church Stretton the valley soon opens out, and at the next town, Craven Arms, the hills are lower and more distant. Craven Arms takes its name from the 17th century inn that once stood almost in isolation at the cross-roads in this valley. With the arrival of the railways in 1840, the inn found itself at a major junction of lines, and around it a town developed to facilitate transhipment of cattle and sheep from the mountains. This relatively new town is not blessed with great architectural merit, although there is an 'old quarter' and the inn itself dates from around 1830. Nevertheless it has a superb setting beside the little River Onny, and has so many interesting attractions that it is advisable to get one of its 'passports' for discounts (see P.48).

Craven Arms is not only a rail junction but also a road junction, and although the A49 continues south to Ludlow, you can turn east to Much Wenlock, or west along the valley of the Clun.

Taking first the Much Wenlock road, the B4368 runs through gentle Corve Dale, dominated by the rising bulk of Brown Clee to the east. Diversions on this side include the pretty village of **Diddlebury** with its brook, 'Diddle Pond', and church with Saxon herringbone stonework in its north wall and a Saxon north doorway. On the opposite side of the B4368, a turning after Broadstone leads down into lonely Hope Dale and the 16th century **Wilderhope Manor**. Austere and isolated, it now finds a role as a Youth Hostel, although it is owned by the National Trust and welcomes visitors on certain days. Back

---

Walking on the Long Mynd

Many people get no farther than the lower end of the Carding Mill Valley, where children can paddle in the crystal-clear stream, and there are grassy acres on which to set out the picnic rugs. But try at the very least to get up to Lightspout Waterfall (about ½ hour each way, described in the NT leaflet), a great favourite of the Victorians, who described its 13foot fall as a 'miniature Niagara'! The NT leaflet also details a round 5-mile walk taking you to the summit at Pole Bank, and a copy of the relevant OS map will reveal many more interesting possibilities. Another resource for walkers is the farmhouse of Thresholds (NW of Craven Arms, off the minor road from Ratlinghope). From Easter to November the farmhouse is open as a walkers' shelter, with displays on the local area and books and maps for sale. Other activities on offer range from guided walks to making corn dollies and indulging in murder mysteries (www.thresholdscentre.co.uk)

It is also worth noting that a shuttle bus service operates between Church Stretton and Bridges in the summer months, so it is possible to get a ride to the top of the Long Mynd and then simply walk back down! Alternatively you can stay on the shuttle to complete the circuit of the mountain.

Spend a day (or more) at Craven Arms!

How much time would you need to do justice to what follows? The Secret Hills Centre is a must, as is a glance at Stokesay Castle, and the Land of Lost Content is unique, to say the least. The Working Farm and Play Barn are both perfect for families of all ages.

The Secret Hills Discovery Centre

This curious establishment just south of the town centre was built by an architect seemingly averse to straight lines. Hardly a one is to be found in this flat-topped grass-roofed building, so blending with the landscape that it would be easy to overlook it – if it were not for the big purple signs! Secret Hills is set in meadowland beside the river and is the starting point of many excellent walks and cycle rides, and even offers an exciting geocaching adventure. Inside, its shop (books, maps, gifts) and cafeteria are freely open to all, while for a small sum you can continue into the circular corridors of the exhibition area and learn everything there is to know about the history, geography and geology of this part of the world. The highlight is a simulated balloon trip over the Shropshire Hills, swooping over ranges like the Long Mynd and Stiperstones and getting a close look at the outlines of the many hill forts of the area.

Open daily from 10am - 4.30pm in winter, 10am – 5.30pm in summer.

The Land of Lost Content

Taking its name from a line of 'A Shropshire Lad', this extensive private collection of 20th century memorabilia is housed in the Old Market Hall. Three floors are utterly crammed with things that you, your mother, or your grandmother might remember from childhood – household items,

toys, films, clothes, food and drink and the rest. Coffee shop overlooks the ground floor.

Open every day except Wednesday 11am – 5pm. Closed January and December

Acton Scott Working Farm

This farm is managed as it would have been more than a hundred years ago, with shire horses, vintage farm machines and hand milking. Children enjoy meeting the animals and there is a café with fresh home-cooked food for resuscitation.

6 miles north of Craven Arms, signed from A49. Open from 11am – 5pm, Easter to end October. Closed Mondays and Bank Holidays

Mickey Miller's Play Barn

A covered area with family activities ranging from toddler games and ball pits to a 21foot death-drop slide. Refreshment area.

1 mile west of Craven Arms on road to Clun. Open school holidays daily 10am – 6pm; term time weekends 10am – 6pm, Wednesday and Thursday 10am – 3pm, Friday 10am – 7pm

Stokesay Castle

Stokesay Castle is actually a fortified manor house, and is deemed the best-preserved example of such in all England. It was built by successful wool merchant Lawrence of Ludlow at the end of the 13th century, and Edward I himself gave Lawrence permission to 'crenellate' his new abode! The great hall, with its fine open fireplace, steep staircase and timber roof has survived unaltered since that time, and there are other interesting features such as the medieval tiled floor in the north tower. Most eye-catching is the superb half-timbered gatehouse with its fine wood carvings. It was added in 1640,

shortly before the 'castle' was surrendered without battle to the Parliamentarian forces.

1 mile south of Craven Arms off A49. Open April to September every day 10am – 5pm; October and March every day except Monday and Tuesday (but open Bank Holidays) 10am – 5pm; rest of year Thursday to Sunday only 10am – 4pm

on the road to Much Wenlock again, you might also like to pause at **Shipton Hall**, a much grander Elizabethan mansion with a Georgian stable block and 13th century dovecote alongside. Visiting times are again limited (see end of chapter).

Much Wenlock

Much Wenlock traces its history back to the 7th century when warmongering Penda, King of Mercia, was extending his domain on all fronts. Penda was definitely Pagan (and is often called 'The Last Pagan King of England'), but without exception his many sons converted to Christianity. One of these, Merewalh, was made ruler of Magonset, the area that now approximates to Shropshire and Herefordshire – and he celebrated his new faith by building a monastery and installing his devout daughter Milburga as Abbess. Though that abbey later fell to marauding Danes, from its ruins a new establishment arose. Wenlock Priory passed into the hands of the Cluniacs after the Norman conquest, and remained so until the Dissolution of the Monasteries in 1536. Today its peaceful ruins on the outskirts of town are in the care of English Heritage.

Much Wenlock itself grew up around the abbey to service the needs of the monks, and received its borough charter in 1468. It continued to thrive, and at one time comprised several townships and returned two MPs to Parliament. Cut down to size when government reorganisation removed its borough status in 1966, it has become a quiet backwater – but one absolutely packed with interesting buildings with stories to tell. If you have the time, it is well worth getting hold of the route of the Much Wenlock Walk from the Tourist Office in The Square (or from www.muchwenlockguide.info) – if not, at least make sure you take a look at the fine 16th century half-timbered Guildhall with its whipping post, haunted Raynald's Mansion on the High Street and Holy Trinity Church that once served the priory. You could add the delightful little town museum, St Milburga's Well (the water is good for finding husbands), Wenlock Pottery and a few antique and book shops before repairing to one of the excellent hostelries for lunch.

Much Wenlock sits behind the wooded escarpment of Wenlock Edge. To the north, the Edge continues to Ironbrdge, with 16th century **Benthall Hall** (off the Broseley Road) worth a visit. Benthall now belongs to the National Trust as indeed does much of the Edge itself. South of Much Wenlock, the Church Stretton road runs along the rim of the Edge with car parks giving access on the way. The best of these is at Presthope, from where there are views across the valleys to the Stretton Hills and three woodland walks are clearly signed.

Once again at the road junction in Craven Arms, the road heading west leads into the gentle valley of the Clun, where Housman's words will once more be drumming in your ears

Clunton and Clunbury,
Clungunford and Clun
Are the quietest places
Under the sun.

Certainly this road is a quiet one passing through a timeless landscape, but it seems that in this case the poet was simply reiterating a local rhyme, in which the adjective could be varied at will. Don't let that thought disturb your enjoyment of this beautiful valley though – glance across the fields to **Clunbury**'s squat church and clustered houses, and at **Clunton** maybe divert north to visit the old hill fort of Bury Ditches. Eventually the road is running beside the river itself, with the pretty picnic spot of Waterloo signed to the left before you arrive at the charming little town of Clun.

Clun

Can any town in England be farther off-the-beaten-track than Clun? With a population of merely 700, it is nevertheless officially a town because it was granted a charter in the 14th century. But Clun goes back a lot farther than that. The Saxons settled here around a church to the south of the river, while later the Normans built a castle on a prominent mound on the opposite bank. Fostered

And Much Wenlock founded the modern Olympic Games

It did, really! The idea was that of a sternly-whiskered Victorian GP by the name of Dr William Penny Brookes. Dr Brookes was always keen to find healthy pursuits to keep his patients out of the public houses, and in 1850 organised the 'First Wenlock Olympian Games'. It was a blend of athletics, traditional sports like cricket and football, and fun events such as a wheelbarrow race and an 'old woman's race'. In 1877, Brookes' request for a special cup to present on the Queen's Jubilee Year brought him into contact with the Greek Chargé d'Affaires in London. Brookes revealed to him his vision for a revival of the original Athenian Olympics, but Greece was unable to respond at the time. In 1889, the doctor (then 80 years of age) contacted French Baron Pierre de Coubertin, who was organising an International Congress on Physical Education. The Baron visited the Wenlock Games, and discussed with Dr Brookes the possibility of an Olympic revival. Much Wenlock is proud to record that in the December issue of 'La Revue Athlétique' the Baron wrote 'If the Olympic Games that Modern Greece has not yet been able to revive still survives today, it is due, not to a Greek, but to Dr W P Brookes'. Seven years later the first of the modern Olympic Games series was held in Athens (1896). Dr Brookes was listed as an honorary member of the Congress, but sadly died four months before the event itself.

In 1994, Juan Antonio Samaranch, then president of the International Olympic Congress, laid a wreath at Dr Brookes' grave in Much Wenlock, saying he 'came to pay homage and tribute to Dr Brookes, who really was the founder of the modern Olympic Games'.

Today an 'Olympic Trail' starts from the Tourist Office in Much Wenlock. Marked out by bronze discs in the ground, this 2km walk visits all the sites associated with the Olympic story.

Wenlock Edge

On Wenlock Edge the wood's in trouble

His forest fleece the Wrekin heaves

The gale, it plies the saplings double

And thick on Severn snow the leaves.

Romantically-named Wenlock Edge drew from Housman these superbly evocative lines, and inspired Vaughan Williams's song cycle of the same name. An 18-mile long limestone escarpment, the Edge spans eastern Shropshire from Craven Arms to Ironbridge. Fossils confirm that it started life as a coral reef in tropical seas, before upheavals moved it north, and collision of continents buckled the rock strata to a 10 degree slope. The shallower dip slope affords good agricultural land and several limestone quarries, while the steep scarp is clothed in ancient deciduous woodland. For part of its length, softer underlying rock has caused this scarp to split, giving rise to the fertile valley known as Hope Dale, sandwiched between wooded crests.

Today the Edge is important for its vegetation and its wildlife – lime-loving bee orchids, birds of prey and Shropshire's largest colony of dormice. Many good paths are maintained through the woodland, and from Presthope a 2-mile circular walk will take you to Lea Quarry, where fossils of ancient sea creatures can be found.

Carding Mill Valley

Guildhall and church, Much Wenlock

Wenlock Priory

Benthall Hall

Town Museum, Much Wenlock

Wilderhope Manor

by the incumbent Fitzalan family, who also owned more-prestigious Arundel Castle, the new town grew up around the stronghold. Nearby the shallow river was spanned, and the narrow packhorse bridge that was put in place in the 15th century still stands and carries traffic today. The castle has fared less well, with no more than a section of the keep and the bases of two towers now to be seen, but its grassy banks offer a splendid picnic site.

Beside the packhorse bridge is a small car park, and from there you can cross a footbridge to stroll around the castle, or walk up into the town to explore. The small shops of the High Street belong to another age. Among them look out for the 17th century stone Malt House (now occupied by a craftsman woodcarver, while his wife runs the atmospheric tearoom next door), and then turn up Hospital Lane to cast an eye on the fine still-in-use almshouses from around the same period. The original twelve residents here were required to say daily

Bury Ditches

There are many, many hillforts in Shropshire, but this is one of the most substantial. The whole area was covered in pine forest until 1978, when a particularly severe gale blew down some trees on the summit. The Forestry Commission decided to remove the rest – and so was revealed this splendid fort with four huge banks of ramparts on the north side and two on the south. From a parking area 2 miles north of Clunton, a track leads uphill to enter the fort by one of its ancient gateways. An orientation table has been installed on the summit and the view includes most of the Shropshire ranges, with the twin Clee hills dominating in the east.

Around the fort, three walking routes have been marked out by posts bearing bands of different colours. All give the chance to explore the ramparts, but children – and the young at heart – will enjoy the game suggested on the display board in the car park. Along the shortest 'blue' route there are four pieces of Iron Age 'treasure' to be found, and you will need sharp eyes!

prayers and to keep respectable hours. Their chapel is open to visitors, as is a part of the gardens, where two of the most characterful tenants have been captured in bronze-like Jemonite by local sculptor Jemma Pearson.

Should you wish to explore farther, St George's Church, on the south side of the river, is set among aged yews and is thought to be on the site of a very ancient place of worship. Playwright John Osborne is buried in the churchyard.

For a drive on the wild side, continue up the Clun valley towards Anchor on the Welsh border. After crossing the river at Newcastle, you have the infant river on your left all the way up to the moorland where it has its source. If your drive needs a destination, turn right at the Anchor Inn, following Forestry Commission signs to a car park in Ceri (or Kerry) Woods. In this isolated spot you have reached the Kerry Ridgeway, an ancient drover's road, and can see it heading east across the hills towards Bishop's Castle. A display board on the site gives more information.

Clun Green Man Festival

In keeping with its rustic nature, Clun's three days of May Day celebration include the likes of mummers, jugglers, stilt-walkers and Morris dancers cavorting through the town. The last day sees the arrival of the Green Man, who firmly defeats Queen Frost on the town bridge. Hundreds pour in to tiny Clun to enjoy the spectacle and everyone then goes on to a final celebratory May Fair in the castle grounds.

To the south of Clun the Welsh border is a mere 8 miles away on the River Teme. **Knighton,** the town that straddles the river, is mainly in Herefordshire, with just its railway station and a few streets in Shropshire. The town is a great walking centre, being at the mid-point of the Offa's Dyke Path and at the start of the Glyndwr's Way that winds west through the border hills. A very different claim to fame is the Spaceguard Centre perched on the hillside above town. Designed to investigate threats of asteroid or comet impact, it is part of an international network, and is open to visitors daily.

From Knighton a minor road makes its way north of the river to rural hamlets like Bucknell, Bedstone and Hopton Castle, nestling beneath the forested hills. Those hills are a Mecca for mountainbikers, who have 20 miles of woodland track and colour-coded trails from beginner to competition standard provided. **Hopton Wood Mountain Bike Trails** can be accessed from a car park off the road west of Hopton Castle.

From Hopton Castle it is possible to return to Hopton Heath and then bend north to **Clungunford.** The adjacent hamlet of Abcott is surprisingly home to one of England's top tea rooms. Swathed in wisteria, Rocke Cottage (formerly The Bird on the Rock) offers the décor, music and costume of the 30s to accompany the delicately cut sandwiches and the very best of home baking.

At Clungunford the Clun has changed direction and is hurrying south to join the Teme. You must go south too – and then follow the main road that meets the Teme on the outskirts of Ludlow, Betjeman's 'loveliest town'.

Hopton Castle

While in the village of Hopton Castle you might cast an eye on the castle itself, beside the road junction. No sign boards announce this forgotten ruin on private land but it has a story to tell. In the Civil War a group of 30 Parliamentarians defended it for three weeks against a 500-strong Royalist force. Finally told that they would be spared if they surrendered, they walked out - only to be killed on the spot. Their spirits, and that of one of their wives, are said to haunt the castle today. Locals give it a wide berth!

Ludlow

Oh come you home of Sunday
When Ludlow streets are still
And Ludlow bells are calling
To farm and lane and mill

Already mentioned in the Domesday Book, Ludlow's road to prosperity began when William the Conqueror gave the land to his henchman, Walter Lacy, and Walter's son Roger set out to build a castle on the bluff above the River Teme. Much later that castle came into the possession of the Crown, and under Edward IV it achieved great importance as the headquarters of his new Council of the Marches of Wales. Royalty made frequent visits to flourishing Ludlow, and the future King Edward V spent his childhood here before his untimely accession and subsequent disappearance in the Tower.

Meanwhile, outside the castle gates, the town itself was prospering through its trade in wool and cloth, generated by the sheep farms of the nearby Welsh hills.

Wealthy merchants built their houses in Ludlow, alongside those of the diplomats and lawyers associated with the Council of the Marches. Several of these early fine buildings remain, but most famous is the timber-framed, lavishly carved Feathers Hotel, built by lawyer Rees Jones in 1619. The 'Feathers' are the ostrich feathers of the Prince of Wales' plume, and though worn by time, they can still be distinguished on the gables.

In the 17th century the cloth industry began to decline in Ludlow, and in 1689, William and Mary abolished the Council of the Marches. The castle, no longer in use, became derelict, but the markets remained, and somehow the town itself thrived and expanded. Fine Georgian houses appeared in the streets leading down to the river, the castle was bought by the Earl of Powis in 1811, and Ludlow became the handsome town it is today.

Other fine buildings in Ludlow include the Buttercross (1744, and once a butter market) and St Laurence's Church at the top of the town. St Laurence's is the largest church in Shropshire, and boasts curiously carved misericords, interesting stained-glass windows and a historic ring of bells. A E Housman's ashes are buried in its grounds beneath a cherry tree (his 'loveliest of trees') and a tablet records his own words:

Goodnight. Ensured release
Imperishable peace.
Have these for yours.

Though very well-rooted in the past, Ludlow is now turning its face to the future. In 2003 it became the first town in Britain to join the Cittaslow movement, an international organisation whose Italian title translates as 'Slow

Clun Green Man

Sculptures at Trinity Almhouses, Clun

Town'. Whatever its name, Cittaslow has little to do with taking things easy, and more to do with promoting local business, craft, food, hospitality and the quality of life in general. Ludlow evidently subscribes to these ideals, and its ancient streets are peopled with traditional butchers, bakers, ironmongers and clothiers, while its restaurants and tearooms proudly announce that they are serving local produce whenever possible. The town annually stages an imaginative Food and Drink Festival, and on its outskirts (2m N on the A49), a new Ludlow Food Centre has opened, selling only locally produced fare. 'Dirty' carrots and 'sleeveless' cucumbers are proving very popular, along with bread baked on the premises and a restaurant that does justice to it all.

Top of Broad Street, Ludlow

Castle at Clun

Ludlow Food Festival - The Sausage Trail

A E Housman

Alfred Ernest Housman (1859-1936) was born in Worcestershire, the eldest of seven children of a Bromsgrove solicitor. After attending the local school he won a scholarship to St John's College, Oxford, but through concentrating only on that part of his studies that interested him, failed to achieve a degree. Ten years as a white collar worker followed, after which he returned to academy and was appointed Professor of Latin at University College London and subsequently Kennedy Professor of Latin at Trinity College, Cambridge.

Although Housman wrote several other volumes of poetry, A Shropshire Lad has always been his most acclaimed work. It was written in the latter years of the 19th century and first published at Housman's own expense, since no publishing house would accept it. At the time the work was begun, Housman had not even visited Shropshire - for him it merely represented a rural idyll, an imagined paradise on the doorstep of his childhood. His descriptions certainly contain some muddled geographical detail!

Housman's poems were quickly seized upon by the composers of the day and Arthur Somervell, George Butterworth, John Ireland and Ralph Vaughan Williams among others set stanzas from A Shropshire Lad to music. By the time of the Great War it had become well known, and its preoccupation with the transitory nature of existence struck a poignant chord with the nation. In later years Housman was a more frequent visitor to Shropshire and though he died in Cambridge, his ashes were brought back to Ludlow for burial. Today, Ludlow's Housman Society meets frequently, and can offer you a 'Housman Trail', a 40-mile drive visiting many of the locations mentioned in his poetry.

Looking out over Ludlow

Take a Walk

The very best view of Ludlow is from Whitcliffe Common on the other side of the river. At the castle gate, take the descending path winding to the right, cross Dinham Bridge and follow the signs to climb uphill through the woods on the opposite side. Bear left to reach the grassy plateau with its toposcope.

Returning to the lower level, you can continue on the riverside path (known as the Breadwalk) downstream as far as the next bridge at Ludford. Here you can cross the river, enter the town through Broad Gate and walk up handsome Broad Street to return to the castle.

The whole route should take you no longer than an hour (unless seduced by the riverside patio at the Charlton Arms beside Ludford Bridge).

Those wanting more than this short stroll can continue up the road from the Common to reach Whitcliffe Woods, part of the Mortimer Forest. Here the Forestry Commission has marked out several colour-coded trails – but the most ambitious might like to extend from Whitcliffe across the deep Mary Knoll Valley to the wooded heights of High Vinnals.

Ask at the Tourist Office for details of marked routes.

Places to Visit

Tourist Information Centres

Bishop's Castle ☎ 01588 638467

Church Stretton ☎ 01694 723133

Craven Arms ☎ 01588 676000

Much Wenlock ☎ 01952 727679

Clun ☎ 01588 640220 (garage on High Street)

Ludlow ☎ 01584 875053

Places of Interest

Snailbeach Mine Visitor Centre

Open Sun and Bank Holidays in summer (approx. May to Oct). Short mining tours available whenever the mine is open. Longer touts on Heritage Day in Sept.

The Bog Visitor Centre

Open mid-Mar to end Oct, 10–5pm every day in school holidays, Wed to Sun and Bank Holidays in term time. ☎ 01743 792484

Bishop's Castle

Bishop's Castle Museum

Open Easter to Oct Sat, Sun and Bank Holidays 1–5pm. ☎ 01588 630007

Bishop's Castle Railway Museum

Open Easter to Oct, Sat, Sun and Bank Holidays 2–5pm ☎ 01588 636446

Craven Arms

Opening details of all attractions around Craven Arms are given on P.48

Clun

Clun museum

Open Easter to Oct Tue 2–5pm; Sat, Bank Holiday Mon and Tue 11am–1pm, 2–5pm.

Shipton Hall

Open Easter to Sept, Thur and Bank Holiday Sun and Mon only 2.30–5.30pm.
☎ 01746 785225

Much Wenlock

Much Wenlock Museum

Open Apr to Sept Mon to Sat 10.30am–1pm, 2–5pm (no lunch break Jun to Aug).
☎ 01952 727773

Wenlock Priory

Open May to Aug daily 10am–5pm; Mar, Apr, Sept, Oct Wed to Sun and Bank Holidays 10am–5pm; Nov to Feb Thur to Sun 10am–4pm.
☎ 01952 727466

Ludlow

The Castle

Open Oct to Mar, daily 10am–4pm (weekends only in Jan); Apr to Jul and Sept 10am–5pm daily; Aug 10am–7pm.
☎ 01584 873355

Ludlow Food Centre

Open Mon to Sat, 9am–5.30pm; Sun 10.30am–4.30pm.
☎ 01584 856000

Knighton

Offa's Dyke Centre

Open Easter to Oct daily 9am–5.30pm; Nov to Easter Mon to Fri only 9am–5pm.
☎ 01547 528753

Spaceguard

Open Wed to Sun and Bank Holidays, tours start at 10.30am, 2pm and 4pm (and last approx 1½ hours).
☎ 01547520247

Best Walks

* Whether you're a seasoned hiker or a Sunday afternoon stroller, you MUST get to the top of Stiperstones; you MUST walk up the Carding Mill Valley; and you MUST peer down from Wenlock Edge. After that you can do what you want – and there's plenty of choice!

* There are so many long-distance trails in this area. The Offa's Dyke Path skirts the borderland, Knighton sees the start of Glyndwr's Way, the Kerry Ridgeway leaves from Bishop's Castle, Ludlow begins the Mortimer Trail, Wild Edric's Way takes the indirect route from Church Stretton to Ludlow, and the 136-mile circular Shropshire Way seems to get just about everywhere.

* The Shropshire Hills (Secret Hills) Centre in Craven Arms offers excellent leaflets on four local circular walks ranging from 2 to 8½ miles in length. It also stocks a comprehensive range of books detailing walks throughout Shropshire. Other particularly walk-orientated centres include the Offa's Dyke Centre at Knighton and Threshold

Continued Over Page

Farm near Church Stretton. But then every Tourist Office in this area is stacked with maps and leaflets to get you out walking.

On your bike

* South Shropshire District Council has produced three superb leaflets of circular cycle rides in this area. Four routes of varying length and difficulty start from Bishop's Castle, a further four from Church Stretton and four more from Ludlow. The leaflets are free and are readily obtained from any Tourist Information Centre. A further leaflet describes the Six Castles Cycleway, a linear route from Shrewsbury to Leominster.

* The website www.shropshirecycling. co.uk is an excellent resource. From this it is possible to download many short circular routes throughout Shropshire.

* Remember that Bridleways are also appropriate for all-terrain bikes (and for walkers, come to that). The Kerry Ridgeway runs 15 miles west from Bishop's Castle and the 100-mile long Jack Mytton Way takes in the Clee Hills, Church Stretton and the Clun Valley

* Hopton Forest has something to offer mountain bikers of all standards, from a simple family circuit to a serious 'black' downhill run.

For the Family

* **Climb a 'mountain'.** Corndon hasn't got the big name of the Long Mynd or Stiperstones but it looks more of a mountain and there's a splendid view from the top. It should take less than ¾ hour from Mitchell's Fold car park to the summit

* **Geocaching at Secret Hills (Craven Arms).** The game is to find treasure – pots of trinkets with child-appeal – hidden in the Shropshire hills. Travel can be by car or by bike, but some final walking and hunting is always involved. For a small sum (and deposit), the Discovery Centre will explain all, and equip you with simple maps and a hand-held GPS unit. Great family fun!

* **Bury Ditches.** The hill fort is interesting and you can involve the children by getting them to look out for the four 'missing' Iron Age artefacts. The sign board at the entrance tells you what to look for and sets it in context.

* **Acton Scott Historic Farm.** Animals, craftsmen in action and quizzes and special activities for younger ones.

A rainy day?

Secret Hills Discovery Centre. Enjoy some virtual fine weather on the air balloon ride, learn all you can about the Hills for later, and indulge in the restaurant while waiting for the skies to clear.

The Land of Lost Content (Craven Arms). Time will pass very quickly here – and the mid-floors cafeteria means you can stay indoors all day.

Church Stretton Antiques Market. With 60 dealers under one roof there's sure to be something here that you've always wanted! Tea room/cafeteria on site.

Go shopping in Ludlow. Enjoy the wealth of individual shops and don't be afraid to go in because everyone here has time for you (it's part of the Cittaslow ethic). A choice of really excellent inns and restaurants for lunch completes the day.

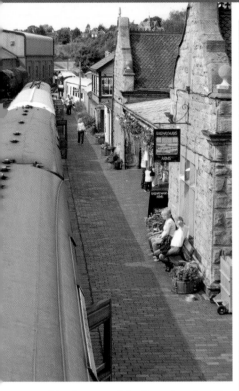

with hamlets and villages often unannounced by name. A good map is a worthwhile investment for venturing here, and the rewards are enormous – unexpected roadside manors, handsome half-timbered farmhouses, and a wealth of churches from Norman times and even earlier.

At the banks of the Severn the scene changes. Bridgnorth spills down a sandstone cliff to the river, and is a town packed with history and curiosity. Charles I handed the town a never-to-be-forgotten compliment when he described the view from the castle on the bluff as 'The finest in all my kingdom'. Clearly he had been missing out on a few places, but the town with its river bridge backed by wooded cliffs is certainly a splendid prospect. From Bridgnorth the sandy-banked river rolls south to leave the county at its south-east tip, where the first oaks and beeches of the Wyre Forest offer picnic sites and woodland walks.

To the east of Ludlow rise the Clee Hills. Brown Clee at 540m is Shropshire's highest peak, but the hill wears the distinction lightly with no drama to its outline and twin summits that are barely distinguishable at a distance. Five miles to the south, Titterstone Clee lacks 7m on its brother, yet its sloping cut-away form is more distinctive – albeit that the contours are in part man-made. Both hills have been extensively quarried over many years.

Around the hills and east to the Severn the countryside is quintessential rural Shropshire. Rolling rich agricultural land is criss-crossed by one-track lanes with high hedges, and scattered

The Clee Hills and 'Cleobury Country'

Leaving Ludlow for the east, the distinctive peak of **Titterstone Clee** (often called simply The Clee) is looming ahead, and the A 4117 climbs steadily to 380m on the bleak moorland of its lower slopes. There is a fine view from this road, but an even finer one from the summit. To access it, you will need to look out for the signed left turn, well before the village of Clee Hill. The narrow road leads to a

Mining on the Clee Hills

Iron ore, clay, lime, coal and stone have been extracted from the Clee Hills since the Middle Ages. In the 1800s, coal was the most important output, and Brown Clee was the highest coalfield in England. Later, the hard stone of the hills (a black basalt known as dhustone or dolerite) was commissioned for the building of Cardiff docks. It was also found to be useful for cobbling roads, and on Titterstone Clee, three quarries opened up to meet the demand. Stone quarrying and coal mining had both ceased on Brown Clee by the mid-1900s, but on Titterstone Clee one quarry is still operational, producing stone that is now used for roadbuilding.

parking area with a precipitous view, from where it is necessary to continue on foot through terrain scattered with the debris of quarrying, and more latterly embellished with the masts and domes of the National Aircraft Tracking System. But ignore the immediate scene and look farther afield. Out there everything from the Malverns to the Black Mountains and the Brecon Beacons is under your gaze – and if you can't sort out all those peaks there is an excellent toposcope back down on the main road again, just past the village of Clee Hill. Almost opposite the toposcope, the solitary house on the corner of the road to the current quarry was once the quarry offices. Now given a facelift, it has become a teashop as well-supplied, comfortable and homely as any you might find in a town street.

East of Clee Hill the road descends

to the town of **Cleobury Mortimer**, whose name is pronounced 'Clibbury' by local residents. Sadly heavy traffic rumbles through its main street, which would otherwise be a pleasant place to investigate the interesting individual shops and several hostelries. The town's most notable feature is the twisted wooden spire of St Mary's Church. Caused by the warping of the old oak beams, this twist is far from a problem, but rather has elevated the town to membership of the exclusive European Twisted Spires Association (of which it there are only three English representatives). In fact St Mary's has another aberration in that the church walls lean outwards at a rather unconventional angle – you may even think there isn't a vertical line in the place. In 1790 Thomas Telford himself was called in to ensure the building's future stability and so far so good!

From Cleobury Mortimer, postman Simon Evans' round (see P.63) took him north as far as **Stottesdon**, a lovely village, and one whose church is well worth a visit. The richly carved font here is classically Norman, the best of its kind in Shropshire. Even older (pre-Conquest) is the west door, now curiously tucked away behind the organ. Its remarkable tympanum has beasts both upside down and standing (possibly a depiction of the chase), presided over by a stern bearded face at the apex.

From Stottesdon it is only about 5 miles to **Cleobury North**, at the foot of Brown Clee, but take care to follow the signs, because the tangled lanes here will have you at their mercy. Once at the village, **Brown Clee** is best accessed by taking the Ditton Priors road followed by an early turn to Abdon. This road soon runs along the foot of the mountain, where there is a parking area and on the opposite side of the road, a field designated as a picnic site. From the end of the picnic field a path leads through the woods to **Abdon Burf**, the 'highest summit' of Brown Clee (Clee Burf, the lower peak, is just south). It will take an hour or a little more to get to Abdon Burf, but the view from Shropshire's loftiest perch makes it all worthwhile. Radio masts and quarrying remains need to be ignored, but the newly-installed toposcope is a great means of identifying all the surrounding features, including the hill fort of Nordy Bank close by in the south-west.

Back at the foot of the hill again, the narrow road runs on to Abdon and continues to the sleepy hamlet of **Tugford**. The handful of houses are gathered around a squat church whose nave, at least, is Norman. Sheila-na gig figures, (see P.64) much worn with time, are perched on either side of the south door on the inside.

From Tugford you might like to brave the threadlike lanes south past Bouldon to **Heath**, where a classically Norman chapel sits alone, surrounded by the humps and hollows that are all that remain of its village. To see inside the chapel you will need to collect the key from the farm up the road. Pulpit, box pews and other features are 17th century.

To the north of Tugford the next village is **Holdgate**, where the church boasts perhaps the best of the Sheila-na-gig figures, on the outside of the south wall of the chancel. The nave is again Norman, as is the handsomely carved font and there is a particularly fine south door. From the churchyard, the view across the valley to Brown Clee is a classic.

The road through Holdgate soon joins the B4368 heading for Bridgnorth. Before reaching that impressive town,

A postman's life

Cleobury Mortimer is proud of its association with Simon Evans, a postman in the town in the years following the Great War. Simon Evans had served on the front and had suffered both physical injuries and gassing. After post-war surgery, he secured a post at Cleobury, where his daily round was a long walk up the valley of the Rea Brook. His damaged lungs recovered a little in the fresh country air and he began to compose poetry and articles on countryside themes for the local press. Eventually he was invited to broadcast on the BBC, which he did regularly for some years, and in time four collections of his articles and a novel were published. Despite his new-found fame Simon Evans continued to live in Cleobury Mortimer, which he loved. Sadly the terrible injuries to his lungs finally overcame him and he died at the age of 45.

Today Cleobury Mortimer's Old Post Office bears a plaque saying 'Simon Evans worked here' and the town has devised an 18-mile circular walk following his footsteps through the Rea valley to Stottesdon. Tourist Information and the bookshop in town can offer maps and information.

Highest hills to the banks of the Severn

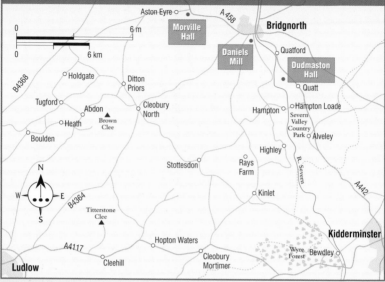

the church at **Aston Eyre** is another worthy of a pause. On a bank above the road, the building is again Norman but its greatest asset is the tympanum above the main door. Said to be the finest piece of Norman carving in Shropshire, it depicts Christ's entry into Jerusalem complete with strewn palms and two donkeys.

A mile east of Aston Eyre (at the junction with the A4580, 3 miles from Bridgnorth) is **Morville Hall**. The handsome Elizabethan grey stone building is in the care of the National Trust and can only be visited by appointment, but beside it is the **Dower House Garden**, developed over 20 years by garden historian Dr Katherine Swift. Cleverly telling the history of Morville Hall and its inhabitants from the early Benedictine monks to the 20th century, it includes a formal Vegetable Garden, Victorian Rose Garden and Canal Garden among others. The garden has featured in many horticultural publications and the whole story

---

Sheila-na-gigs

Sheila-na-gigs are essentially pagan fertility symbols. They were once fairly common on churches throughout the British Isles, but the rather explicit nature of these female figures offended Victorian sensibilities and most were removed at this time. Just 18 remain in England today, of which four are in Shropshire (One on each side of the south door at Tugford, one on the south chancel wall at Holdgate and one above the north door at Church Stretton).

Toposcope on Clee Hill

is told in Katherine Swift's recently published book, *The Morville Hours*. Drive past the house to park beside the Norman church for access.

Bridgnorth

Bridgnorth is a town with a curious situation. Split into two parts by a 100 feet high sandstone cliff on the banks of the river, the local adage 'With its head up in heaven - its toes in the Severn' describes it perfectly! In fact the two parts of the town are quite separate in background. 'High Town' grew up around a 12th century castle that originally belonged to Robert de Bellême, son of Roger de Montgomerie. This part of the town was once fortified, and

Talbot Hotel, Cleobury Mortimer

Brown Clee from Holdgate

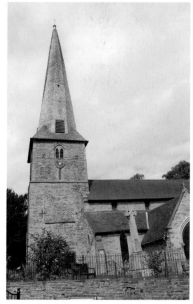

Twisted spire, Cleobury Mortimer

its walls enclosed dwellings, churches, market place and civic buildings. Far below at the foot of the cliff, 'Low Town' was all about trade on the river. Water levels only permitted this for something like eight months of the year (and even then only on certain days), so the wharves were lined with warehouses storing goods awaiting shipment and inns where boatmen passed the long hours of delay. Bridgnorth at one time had three boatbuilding yards, and was said to be the busiest inland port in Europe.

The riverside port area was connected to High Town by just one cobbled road, the Cartway, and by seven sets of steps cut into the sandstone. The cliff itself was riddled with dwelling caves, many of which can still be seen today.

The Civil War altered the face of High Town for ever. The Royalists held the castle, and when Cromwell's troops approached, they defended their stronghold by setting fire to the High Street. Unfortunately things got out of hand and the flames spread to a powder store in St Leonard's Church – after which not a lot was left of Bridgnorth. The Parliamentarians took the castle and decided to blow up its remains in case the Royalists should come back. Just a part of the keep was left, and it is still there today, tilting at an alarming 17° (compare this with the paltry 4° of the Leaning Tower of Pisa).

The town was gradually rebuilt and thrived on trades like malting, tanning and weaving. Hazeldine's iron foundry was established and in 1808, famously turned out the parts for Richard Trevithick's *Catch Me Who Can*, the first steam locomotive to carry fare-paying passengers. The arrival of the railway in 1862 finally transformed both parts of Bridgnorth. On the river trade slowed in favour of more reliable transport, while up above, the walk along the clifftop became fashionable with the new 'tourists', and those with wealth built fine villas to enjoy the views. In 1892 a novel Cliff Railway (operated by water-ballast in tanks beneath the cars) was added to the scene. Three years later, the very last cargo-carrying barge on the Severn sank after hitting a pillar of Bridgnorth bridge.

A Walk around Bridgnorth

All Bridgnorth's history is written in its streets. The Tourist Office offers a fairly comprehensive Town Trail, but a simple short stroll will reveal the best of it – and if it should be summertime, the abundant floral displays are a bonus.

Begin by making your way to turreted Northgate at the top end of the High Street. **Northgate** is the only remaining town gate, and it was last re-built in 1910. Today it houses the town museum, whose collection ranges from Saxon artefacts to a model of Trevithick's high pressure engine. At the crossroads just in front of the Northgate, the road to the left will take you past old almshouses to **St Leonard's Church** at the highest point of the town. Continuing down High Street again, the black and white **Old Town Hall** in the middle of the road was built in 1652, since when it has sheltered many a market stall beneath its arches.

At the end of High Street, turn left to go down the **Cartway**. It looks rather different now from the days when the

Beware the boatmen!

The classic boat was the Severn Trow, a flat-bottomed, keel-less, masted vessel suited to the shallow water. A team of 3 or 4 men would take it downstream with the current, using its square sail to give power for the return. Unfortunately this was often insufficient, and teams of 6 or 8 'bowhauliers' were needed to heave the boat back by means of a rope tied to the top of its mast. Until the late 1700s there was no suitable towpath for horses. This hard unpredictable life meant that all trow men were rough characters - but the strong thickset bowhauliers were the worst. Their pastimes ranged from drinking and womanising to bare-knuckle fighting and bear-baiting. Bridgnorth's riverside was no place to linger in the Middle Ages!

carts and packhorses trundled goods to and from the port, and the rough cottages alongside were lodging houses for the bargees, and inns where they could be 'entertained'. The flower-bedecked Black Boy Inn was once a boatmen's hostelry, while at the bottom, half-timbered **Bishop Percy's House** (1580) was in 1729 the birthplace of academic Thomas Percy. Newspaper editor and compiler of poetry, he became Bishop of Dromore in Ireland.

Going ahead to the road junction, the bridge on the left spanning the Severn was built in 1823 – the clock tower on its far side commemorates Trevithick's nearby achievements. Across the river upstream are the grassy acres of **Severn Park**, the starting point for canoe excursions. But back again at the bottom of the Cartway, continuing ahead along the riverside promenade soon has you at the foot of the **Cliff Railway**. Taking a ride is 'like being lifted up to heaven' according to John Betjeman (how can you resist that?), but Stoneway Steps make the same journey alongside if you really prefer.

At the top of the cliff (by steps or railway), turn left to continue along Castle Walk. This lofty promenade was much beloved by the Victorians – and this was the view that had Charles I so ecstatic. On the right stands handsome classical-style **St Mary's Church,** designed by Thomas Telford, and beyond it, the **Castle Grounds** with bandstand and rich floral displays. At the top corner the old castle keep holds its unlikely posture, making you wonder if it's safe to leave the gardens that way!

Once through the gate, you can quickly walk ahead up elegant Georgian **East Castle Street** back to town, but Bridgnorth has one final attraction, and a very popular one at that. If you turn left at the gate of the gardens, walk down steps and then continue downhill along the road you will soon reach a footbridge vaulting the valley to the Severn Valley Railway Station beneath Panpudding Hill. All year round trains huff and puff the 16 miles south to Kidderminster, and there is no better way to explore this part of the world.

From Brignorth the Severn takes a fairly straight course south-east, and the next crossing for vehicles is some 13 miles away at Bewdley (in Worcestershire). You could confine your explora-

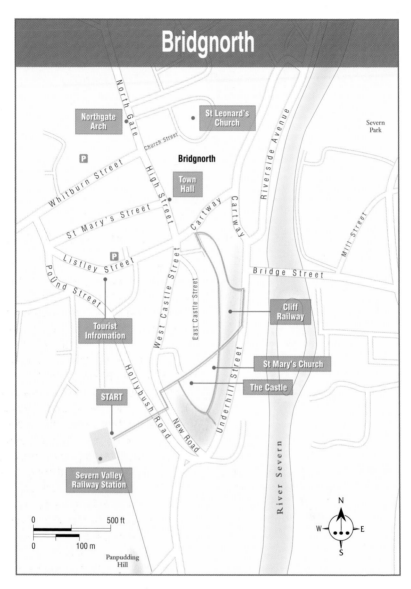

Bridgnorth

tion to either side of the river or take this round tour, which strays over the county boundary.

A circular drive around the Severn Valley (approx. 30 miles)

At the end of Bridgnorth's bridge (beneath the cliff and facing it), turn left along the riverside and then left again on the B4555 (SP Daniel's Mill, Highley). This road parallels the right bank of the Severn, and after a mile or so, reaches **Daniel's Mill**. The restored mill is situated in a steep-sided valley with the Severn Valley Railway crossing high overhead, and it has been

Daniels Mill

Bridgnorth, Severn Valley Railway

The Severn Valley Railway

The original Severn Valley line was closed in 1963, but the Severn Valley Railway Society was very quickly formed, and in 1970, the section from Bridgnorth to Hampton Loade was opened under the new management. Four years later the service was extended to Bewdley, but it was not until 1984 that the line reached Kidderminster. Since then its only major setback has been the damage caused by the violent thunderstorms of 19th June 2007, when large sections of the bank were washed away. Now repaired and back in service, the Severn Valley Railway remains one of the most popular of the restored lines. Its engines are mostly steam (with the occasional diesel), and they run throughout the year, with special events like Thomas the Tank Engine weeks, Jazz journeys and Santa Specials added. In 2008 a new Engine House exhibition centre was opened at Highley station where enthusiasts can get 'hands-on' with the locomotives. Much more information is on www. svr.co.uk

Bridgnorth, High Street with Old Town Hall

Bridgnorth, Cliff Railway

Bridgnorth, Northgate

worked by the same family for six generations. This is a genuine carefully maintained watermill and visits are conducted by the miller himself, with the huge iron wheel and grinding gear set in motion. You can buy some of the freshly-ground wholemeal flour – or enjoy scones made from the same with a cup of tea in the garden.

On now through Eardington and Chelmarsh, after which a sign points left to Hampton. The road descends past the railway station to the Severn, where a chain ferry can take you across to **Hampton Loade** and the River and Rail Inn on the opposite bank. There has been a ferry crossing here for some 400 years but the present model was built in the Ironbridge Gorge Museum and launched in 2004. Like its predecessor, it operates attached to a cable slung across the river, the power being provided by a rudder held at a certain angle to the current.

Back on the B4555 again and the next village, **Highley**, was a coalmining centre until the last shaft closed in 1969. Its streets of terraced cottages, once home to the workforce, are now festooned with flowers, and Highley has been transformed into one of the most attractive villages around. At the end of the village, a road on the left leads down to handsome **Highley Station** on the Severn Valley Railway, with the new **Engine House** nearby (see box). The same road (and the one before it) gives access to the **Severn Valley Country Park**. The park occupies both banks of the river, and there is a footbridge to take you over to the Visitor Centre and café on the far side.

A couple of miles west of Highley (signed from the B4555) is **Rays Farm**, splendid countryside entertainment for all the family. The farm animals here include goats, deer, donkeys, red squirrels, guinea pigs and owls and there are miles of woodland walks where more than 50 magical and mystical wood carvings are hidden. Would-be kings can try their luck at removing the sword Excalibur from its stone! Indoor and outdoor picnic tables and restaurant facilities invite you to spend a whole day.

South of Rays Farm, a left turn in Kinlet takes you through the **Wyre Forest** to Bewdley. In the wood, the first parking place on the right (Earnwood Copse) is the starting point for walks and a fairly demanding mountain bike trail.

Bewdley itself is a delightful town, with splendid old buildings and fine Georgian houses on its riverside. Cross the river bridge, then bear left on theB4190, passing through the suburbs of Kidderminster to join the A442 and head north again. After Shatterford you are once more in Shropshire. At Alveley a turning will take you back to the Severn Valley Park on this east side of the river, and farther on you can likewise access the ferry at Hampton Loade again.

After Quatt, an estate village, **Dudmaston Hall** stands in parkland on the left. 17th century Dudmaston is owned by the National Trust, and its three-day-week opening schedule scarcely does justice to this lovely house and even lovelier gardens. The house is perhaps most remarkable for

Places to Visit

Tourist Information Offices

Bridgnorth:
☎ 01746 763257

Places of Interest

Morville Hall
Visits by appointment only.
☎ 01746 780838

Dower House Garden
Open Apr to Sept, Wed, Sun and Bank Holidays 2–6pm.
☎ 01746 714407

Bridgnorth

Bridgnorth Cliff Railway Railway
Open Summer, Mon to Sat 8am-8pm, Sun 12noon–8pm; Winter: Mon to Sat 8am–6.30pm, Sun 12noon–6.30pm.
☎ 01746 762052/762 124

Northgate Museum
Open Easter to Oct, Sat 1.30–4pm, Sun and Bank Holidays 11am–4pm; During school holidays, everyday except Sat 11am–4pm, Sat 2–4pm.
☎ 01746 762830

* Severn Valley Railway (Bridgnorth to Kidderminster)
For timetables etc,
☎ 01299 409816 or see www.svr.co.uk

Severn Park – Sun Valley Canoeing
Day and weekend trips down the Severn, returning by Severn Valley Railway, starting every day from Apr to Oct.
☎ 07774 907326
www.virtual-shropshire.co.uk/sun-valley-canoeing

Daniel's Mill
Open Apr to Sept, Wed, Sat, Sun 11am–4pm, Bank Holidays 11am–6pm
☎ 01746 762753

Rays Farm Country Matters, Billingsley
Open Feb to Oct everyday 10am–5.30pm.
☎ 01299 841255

Dudmaston Hall
Open Easter to Sept.
Garden: Mon, Tue, Wed, Sun 12noon-6pm; Tea Room: Mon, Tue, Wed, Sun 11.30am–5.30pm; House: Tue, Wed, Sun 2–5.30pm; Shop: Tue, Wed, Sun 1–5.30pm.
☎ 01746 780866

Continued Over Page

its modern art collection, while the grounds include a large lake, woodland dingle and waterfall. It is possible to walk from the house along the riverside to Hampton Loade, a distance of about 1½ miles.

From Dudmaston the return to Bridgnorth through Quatford is un-remarkable – but it is interesting to note that Quatford was in a way the forerunner of Bridgnorth, because Robert de Bellême had his original castle, church and borough here before moving the whole power base north to the more defendable site at Bridgnorth.

Places to Visit

Take a Walk

* The Simon Evans Way is a very good 18 mile ramble (it can easily be shortened) but you will need to follow the booklet very carefully. OS Explorer Map 218 (Wyre Forest and Kidderminster) might help.

* South and north of Bridgnorth, the Severn Way hugs the right bank of the river. To the south, the Severn Valley Railway offers many options for a quick return (Hampton 5 ½ miles, Upper Arley 10 ¼ miles), while to the north it is possible to walk through to Ironbridge (9 miles) and return by bus (Arriva no. 9)

* The Wyre Forest offers lots of walking opportunities. Paths lead out from Earnwood Car Park (on the B4199) for casual rambles. Otherwise waymarked and themed trails leave from the Forestry Commission Visitor Centre on the A456, 3 miles west of Bewdley

On your bike

* The Mercian Way, otherwise known as National Cycle Route 45, makes use of lanes and traffic-free tracks for its 20-mile length between Bridgnorth and Bewdley. Pick up a free leaflet at any Tourist Office.

* The Wyre Forest offers various mountain bike trails. Those suitable for families start from the Wyre Forest Visitor Centre (see Walks section)

* 'The best way to explore Cleobury Country is by bike'! So saying, Shropshire County Council have devised four routes starting from Cleobury Mortimer, ranging from a easy evening ride to the demanding all-day Clee Challenge. Tourist Offices have the leaflet, or the routes can be downloaded from: www.shropshirecycling.co.uk

For the family

* Climb a mountain. Abdon Burf (Brown Clee Hill) is probably the most family-friendly (see text). And it's free!

* Take a ride on the Severn Valley Railway. If you are going the whole way and have more than one child, make sure you get a family ticket - and note that family ticket or whole-distance fare means that you have unlimited travel that day. Highley Engine House costs extra, but is a bonus!

* Rays Farm is delightful for all ages. Most of the woodland walks are suitable for pushchairs or wheelchairs, with just a small section having steps and a bridge.

A rainy day?

* The railway is good for beating the weather, even if the scenery is a little less appealing in the rain. Remember that full-distance fare = unlimited travel, so you could theoretically keep dry all day. Or maybe just take a trip to Highley Engine House where you can linger and watch the trains passing.

* Northgate Museum offers good browsing – and lots of information about Bridgnorth.

* Take a drive to look at the churches. You could follow the route here from Cleobury Mortimer through Stottesdon and around Brown Clee Hill, but you could increase your scope by picking up the leaflet Explore the Churches of the Bridgnorth Area from the Tourist Office at Bridgnorth.

East of Shrewsbury, the tree-clad cone of the Wrekin rises abruptly from the flat agricultural plain. Standing right beside the M54 and A5, Shropshire people have always seen it as a sentinel welcoming them home, and naturally it is not short of attached folk-lore.

Beyond the Wrekin, the new town of Telford straddles the motorway. Travellers see little more than the blue plaza towers shining down on them, but behind is a large shopping complex and an enormous town park with lakes, playground and children's Wonderland. Designated in 1969, Telford is one of the latest 'new towns', and its creation engulfed old boroughs to mingle, not

always easily, with the new.

The territory of Telford extends south to the Severn and the Ironbridge Gorge, and perhaps for this reason the town declares itself the 'Birthplace of Industry'. The events around Ironbridge in the 18th century triggered the Industrial Revolution, and there are now ten individual museums to tell the tale. Crowded, dirty and noisy it must have been, but today visitors are welcomed to a peaceful green valley, picturesquely spanned by the famous iron bridge, and a town with many interesting shops and restaurants.

Farther east still, Shropshire pushes its boundary into Staffordshire. There is plenty to see and do in this midland area – Weston Park is a stately home with many added attractions, White Ladies Priory and Boscobel House chronicle Charles II's escape from his Cromwellian pursuers, Albrighton has a fine rose garden and nearby Cosford is home to an extensive RAF museum.

The Wrekin

The Wrekin is almost the symbol of Shropshire, the spiritual heart of the county. Shropshire people will drink a toast to 'all friends around the Wrekin' and talk about 'going all around the Wrekin' where others might say 'going all around the houses'. As a hill, it is not that high – only 407m – but perhaps some of its fascination is its isolation,

Where did the Wrekin come from?

The textbook explanation is that although the Wrekin was not a volcano, its rock is indeed volcanic dust and lava, thrust to the surface some 600 million years ago. More romantic minds will tell you the story of a giant with a grievance against the people of Shrewsbury, who carried along a shovelful of earth with which to dam the Severn and so flood the town. He apparently asked a cobbler carrying a bag of old shoes how far he had yet to go. The cobbler, seeing the giant's intent, said it was so far that he had worn out all these shoes along the way – whereupon the giant angrily threw down the earth he was carrying, thus creating the Wrekin!

which is even more apparent when seen from a distance.

The Wrekin is a very popular and very straightforward climb, if a little on the steep side! The path starts opposite the carpark under the rocks on the road from the M54 (Junction 7) to Little Wenlock, and continues as an obvious wide track snaking uphill. The view from the top is as stunning as you might expect, and a toposcope details all you can see. The other feature of the summit, the 'Beacon on the Wrekin', is a transmitting station used for broadcasting and telecommunications.

In fact the Wrekin is not quite the only hill around, because standing alongside it is a very minor bump called **the Ercall** (pronounced locally as Arcal). The Ercall has been quarried, and it is a treasure for geologists because in its exposed rock faces, pink and grey rock can be seen side by side. The pink is Pre-Cambrian, dating from a time when life forms were all soft-bodied, and so there are no fossils; the grey is one step farther along the evolutionary line, and is full of the shell fossils of the 'Cambrian explosion'. The quarries are easily visited, and there are four well-marked out walks in the woods around the Ercall.

Telford

In the lee of the Wrekin, Telford was created as an extension of Dawley New Town, which had already been in existence some six years. Along with Dawley, it incorporated the older settlements of Wellington, Oakengates, Madeley and (not without some initial heated discussion), the towns on the north side of the Ironbridge Gorge.

The new town of Telford was given

Is Telford in Shropshire?

In 1974, a new district known as the Wrekin was created within the county of Shropshire. In 1998, now as Telford and Wrekin, it became a unitary authority, its government independent of Shropshire County Council. But it remains in the historic and 'ceremonial' county of Shropshire (a county defined in the 1997 act as having its own Lord Lieutenant) – and the people who live here certainly feel they are Salopians!

Thomas Telford (1757 – 1834)

Thomas Telford was born at Westerkirk, Dumfrieshire, the only son of a shepherd who died the same year. Growing up in poverty, at the age of 14 he was apprenticed to a local stone mason, and from there moved on to Edinburgh, London and Portsmouth. During this time he taught himself the skills of architecture and engineering. Having gained the patronage of wealthy Sir William Pulteney, who came from the same Scottish parish, he secured the post of Surveyor of Public Works in Shropshire - and in doing so found the scope to extend his talents. Telford renovated Shrewbury Castle and refashioned the town's prison, built bridges across the Seven (including an 'iron bridge' at Bridgnorth that used only half as much iron as its predecessor upstream) and designed distinctive churches at Bridgnorth and at Madeley. When the architect for the Shrewsbury Canal died suddenly, he took over that project, and built an impressive iron-troughed aqueduct to cross the river at Longdon-upon-Tern. It stands today, isolated in a field, its story too important for it to be dismantled, but sadly with no access. The Ellesmere Canal (now the Llangollen Canal) was a much bigger undertaking and necessitated his most spectacular work, the Pontcysyllte aqueduct carrying the canal 126ft above the River Dee. Canal architecture finally made Telford's name and he laid his hand on most of the canal networks of Birmingham and the Midlands before moving on to the Caledonian Canal in Scotland, and finally, at the request of the King of Sweden, to the Göta Canal.

Moving back to Scotland, roadbuilding was added to Telford's skills, and more than a thousand miles of highway and a similar number of bridges were his contribution to the country's transport structure. Coming south again, he redesigned the Shrewsbury-Holyhead Road and the North Wales coast road, building the suspension bridges at Conwy and the Menai Straits. By the early years of the 19th century, Telford's works could be seen throughout the length and breadth of Britain and he was one of the great men of his time. Telford was buried in the nave of Westminster Abbey, with an effigy in white marble later placed in nearby St Andrew's Chapel.

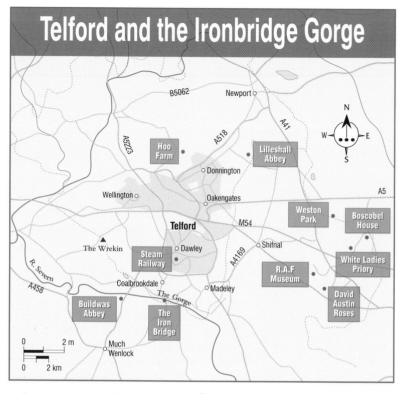

Telford and the Ironbridge Gorge

as its centrepiece a huge shopping complex, which today it is scheduled for a facelift. It is surrounded by vast areas of car park, helpfully colour-coded and labelled (Cherry Pink, Lime Green, Blue Willow, etc) in deference to the disorientating nature of new town landscapes. The only obvious features

on the horizon here are the blue glassy office towers known as Telford Plaza, but by following a few signposts, it is possible to find the Law Courts, in front of which Telford himself, hat in hand, leans ponderously on the letters of his name. It is a scene included in every tourist brochure.

A few more signposts are needed to direct you to the Town Park, which is on the south side of the Shopping Centre. The Park has its own parking lots (signed from the roads) but it can also be easily reached from any of the 'colour' parks around the Centre. The Ten Pin Bowl and Ice Rink (the only one in Shropshire) are near its entrance. **Telford Town Park** is a vast 450 acres of landscaped greenery. With plenty

Wonderland, Telford

Town Park, Telford

Sunnycroft, Wellington

of space for picnics and ball games there are also imaginative children's playgrounds, a pedalo lake, a sensory garden, a vast wild area of lakes, woods and pathways, a collection of Japanese flowering cherries, and – the only one that requires financial outlay – a Wonderland of fairytale figures, accessed by cheerful red 'Teddy's Train'. Telford's planners did well with Town Park, and today it is well cared for, a treat for the family after shopping, or an inexpensive day out in its own right.

Farther afield Telford

North of the M54, **Wellington** stands on the old A5 (Watling Street to the Romans), and is a town that particularly thrived in the Victorian and Edwardian industrial era. Witness to this is the 'Gentleman's villa' **Sunnycroft**,

now in the care of the National Trust, and said to be one of many built for prosperous business men at the time. Wellington's claim to fame is that poet Philip Larkin's first job was at the library here, and the town now hosts an annual Literary Festival.

Like Wellington, Ketley, Oakengates and Donnington have a industrial heritage, standing on the site of previous coal mines and iron works. Beyond and among their streets of terraced houses stand newer developments, becoming ever more affluent towards the limit of the built-up area. To the north-east, and outside the borough of Telford, **Newport** has somehow retained its old market town character, with a wide main street and lovely Early English church. To the south of the town are two places worthy of a visit - **Hoo**

Buildwas Abbey

The Iron Bridge

Farm Animal Kingdom is a family attraction where steeplechasing sheep and galloping goats are the order of the day (as well as the more usual farming pursuits), while farther east, the ruins of the church and cloisters at Lilleshall Abbey are open to all for quiet reflection.

To the south of the M54 is Dawley New Town, and to its west, Horsehay, the location of the **Telford Steam Railway** (a model railway, miniature railway and steam tram are extra diversions on the site). South of them all, **Madeley** is a much older settlement that again prospered in the days of mining, while beyond the land falls steeply to the Ironbridge Gorge.

The Ironbridge Gorge

For three miles or so the Severn flows through a deep gorge, and the settlements along its banks bear witness to their important role in the Industrial Revolution. But before venturing into that gorge, there is one place at its extreme western end that is worth a visit. **Buildwas Abbey** was founded by the Bishop of Coventry in 1135 and first inhabited by a handful of monks from Furness Abbey. The church has remained unaltered since that time, and is intact apart from its roof, making it one of the best-preserved examples of 12th century Cistercian architecture in Britain today. Essentially of simple design, thick Norman pillars impressively flank the wide nave. Other parts of the abbey to have suffered little are the beautifully vaulted and tiled chapter house and an adjacent section of clois-ter. The crypt below the north transept has recently been opened to visitors.

Buildwas marks the start of the Gorge, and following the river downstream from there you soon pass the gigantic cooling towers of the Ironbridge Power Station. When under construction in the 60s, a red pigment was added to the concrete of those towers in order that they should match the colour of the local soil, and the station initially merited listing for a conservation award! With all its perceived architectural merits, the planners were careful enough to place it where it could not be seen from the gorge itself, and a bend in river and road separates the station from the first town, **Coalbrookdale**.

Although its name is less well known than that of neighbouring Ironbridge, it is to Coalbrookdale that the honours for the Industrial Revolution belong. The proximity of coal, wood, minerals and the river made the valley a perfect location for industrialisation, and iron smelting was carried on here from around 1600. In 1709 **Abraham Darby** developed a method for this smelting using coke rather than the formerly-employed charcoal, thus making the metal easier to produce and bringing down the costs involved. Darby's original furnace still stands in the middle of Coalbrookdale, overlooked by the elegant Georgian houses where the family once lived, and with the Museum of Iron alongside to tell the story.

The smelting work was continued by Abraham's son and then his grandson, both also called Abraham. As Quakers they looked after the welfare of their workforce, and walks were laid out through the woods to offer an alternative to leisure time spent in the public houses. An iron 'rotunda' was built at the highest point to give both workers and visitors the best view of the gorge. Over time the Darbys extended their production to that of boats, wheels, iron track for the railways and, in 1779, the world's first iron bridge, crossing the Severn. Individual wooden pieces were used to make the moulds for the iron, and the resulting segments were then fitted together using woodworking techniques such as dovetail joints. The bridge was instantly applauded, and admirers from far and wide descended on 'Ironbridge'.

By this time other related industries had come to the gorge, and it was a scene to behold, particularly at night when the raging furnaces lit up the sky. Wealthy industrialists built their villas high on the wooded banks for the view and the new Tontine Hotel was built at the end of the bridge to accommodate the influx of visitors. The heyday of the Gorge lasted until the second half of the 19th century, when the advent of the railways removed the advantage of the river for transport, and South Wales and the Black Country took over its role. In 1986 Ironbridge Gorge was declared a UNESCO World Heritage site and ten museums relating its former glory have now been opened along the length of the valley (see P.80).

Still celebrating iron but in more modern mode, a further site of interest is the **Open Air Museum of Steel Sculpture**, comprising 10 acres of exhibits on a wooded hillside above Coalbrookdale (turn right after the Museum of Iron). And down near the river in Coalbrookdale is one more fascinating place to visit, the **Green Wood Centre**. Run by the Small Woods Association, it offers courses in woodland management and crafts, but it also boasts a vegetarian wholefoods café, woodland products for sale, and a section devoted to coracle making.

The East

Beyond the houses of Telford, a little 'nose' of Shropshire projects into neighbouring Staffordshire. This is the corner of the county to head for on a rainy day – and maybe on a fine one, too – because there is plenty of interest for all the family within the space of very few miles. Turn south off the M54 at Junction 3, follow signs and you will very quickly find the **RAF Museum at Cosford**. On the edge of an RAF base, it is spread throughout several hangars and is entirely free (although donations are welcome). In addition to the planes, missiles, engines and motor vehicles, there is an exhibition on the Cold War, the adventure of a simulated 'test flight' (the only item that requires payment), the opportunity to match your visual acuity and reaction times against those of RAF pilots and a 'Fun 'n' Flight' interactive section for children.

You could easily spend the whole day at Cosford, but just half a mile farther down the A41 signs lead you off down winding lanes to a very different place of interest, **David Austin Roses**. The blooms waft their scents from the fields on either side long before you reach the Plant Centre. Visitors come from all over the world to this home of English Roses and plenty of staff are always on

Ironbridge is the perfect destination for a rainy day as well as for a fine one, with ten different 'museums' to choose from. A Passport Ticket giving entry to all the museums for a whole year makes a very sound investment – its cost is probably less than two individual admissions.

Museum of the Gorge

This little museum beside the river in Coalbrookdale is the best place to start, because it offers a 10-minute scene-setting video on the history of the Gorge. There is also an interesting 40ft long model of the Gorge as it was in 1795 (complete with 'Severn Trows' on the river), and more obscurely, a few items devoted to industrial impact and recycling.

Museum of Iron

At the Centre of Coalbrookdale (1/2 mile up Dale Road from the Museum of the Gorge), this is a museum on three floors. The centre floor focuses on the valley in its heyday, with a large model of the water courses that supplied the power, a recreation of the inclined plane system, a video and one or two interactive exhibits. Above them the top floor groans with cast ironware displayed at the 1851 Great Exhibition alongside a medley of kitchenware and ranges, and the more recent additions, Aga and Rayburn cookers. The ground floor cafeteria (light lunches and home-made cakes) and bursting-at-the-seams souvenir shop are open to everyone, as is Abraham Darby's original coke furnace, now housed under a permanent canopy in the courtyard.

Enginuity

Close to the Museum of Iron, this hands-on museum is aimed at the younger generation – although it is quite obvious from a look around that it is just as much fun for their parents and grandparents (and of course, the accompanying children are not strictly necessary!). Generate power from the river, build a house that will withstand an earthquake, feed waste to the recycling machine, pull a 5-ton locomotive and lots more – this museum has so many diversions that there should be space for all, even on a wet Bank Holiday Monday!

The Darby Houses.

There was no commuting to work for the Darby family – their Georgian residences are just a stone's throw from the furnace and factories at Coalbrookdale. Original furniture graces the high-ceilinged rooms of Rosehill House, while Dale House boasts the wood-panelled room in which Abraham Darby III designed his famous Iron Bridge.

The Iron Bridge and Toll House

There's no charge for admiring the iron bridge, and in the former toll house a small exhibition tells you exactly how and why it was built. Tourist Information is housed in the same building.

Jackfield Tile Museum

Downstream from the Iron Bridge and on the south side of the river is the village of Jackfield. The tile factory here was established in 1874. Today tiles are still made on the ground floor of the huge brick building, while upstairs a series of rooms recreate classic tiling scenarios – the arched walls and nameplate of a London Underground station, a frieze of sheep and lambs on the back wall of the butcher's shop, a happy maypole dancing scene from a Children's Hospital ward. More tiles invite you to guess their original home, while others are exhibited purely for their style or beauty. A walk through part of the current Craven Dunnill tile factory ends the visit.

Blists Hill Victorian Town

Downstream again, and north of the river, Blists' Hill is the pièce de résistance. By far the biggest 'museum', a few hours are needed to do it justice, and the cost of entry might well make you think about the value of the Passport mentioned at the beginning of this section. Blists Hill comprises a town street of houses, shops, pubs, a bank and craftsmen's workshops, and a large open space occupied by the carousel, coconut shy and other stalls of an old-fashioned fairground. Alongside the latter is a Victorian schoolroom (carefully moved from its original location), an iron foundry, a toll house, and more. Shopkeepers, publicans, fairground workers and the rest wear 19th century costume, and, in keeping, prices everywhere are displayed in pounds, shillings and pence. To join in the spirit of the place you need to change your money in the bank at the entrance, but in practice today's currency is also acceptable.

There should be even more to see at Blists Hill in 2009. Current extensions

Continued over page

include a new side street of shops and houses leading to the towpath of the former canal and a restored inclined plane. A narrow gauge Miner's Railway and a new Visitor Centre are also being added.

Coalport Museum

Not far from Blists Hill but on the riverside is Coalport China Museum. This was the home of the famous Coalport firm until 1926. Now it houses the National Coalport and Caughley collection, a dazzling miscellany of colour and design. The visit includes exhibits on the history of china making, and sometimes also the opportunity to get some hands-on experience in a workshop. The setting itself is most attractive, with a shapely bottle kiln standing beside the duck-friendly Shropshire Canal.

The Tar Tunnel

From Coalport, a short walk along the Shropshire Canal will bring you to the foot of the Hay Inclined Plane that once carried small boats to and from the canal above. The small cottage alongside allows access to the Tar Tunnel. The original shaft was opened up in association with the coal mines, and workers were amazed to find natural bitumen flowing from its walls and collecting in pools on the floor. Cauldrons were set up at the tunnel entrance to boil the bitumen to create pitch to treat ropes and wood. It was even bottled as 'British Oil', a remedy for rheumatism! Put on a hard hat and you can see that even today, a black treacly substance oozes between the bricks of the tunnel walls.

Broseley Pipeworks

A couple of miles south of Ironbridge, you will need to cross the stylish Jackfield Bridge and follow signs through attractive Broseley for this one. White long-stemmed clay pipes enjoyed huge popularity in the latter part of the 19th century. The clay pipe factory in Broseley opened in the 1880s, using china clay imported from Cornwall on the local railway. After the works closed in the 1957 its contents remained virtually undisturbed, and the visit includes a 'time-capsule' section as well as traditional exhibits and videos.

Opening Times

Summer (approx. April to October inclusive)
All museums except Broseley Pipeworks are open every day from 9am–5pm
Broseley Pipeworks is open only from mid-May to mid-Sept at the same times.
Winter (approx Nov to Mar inclusive)
Coalbrookdale's Mueum of Iron, the Museum of the Gorge, the Tollhouse, Jackfield Tile Museum and Coalport China Museum are open every day from 9am–5pm
Blists Hill Victorian Town is open 9am–4pm
The Darby Houses, Broseley Pipeworks and the Tar Tunnel are closed.
All museums are closed Christmas Day, Boxing Day and New Year's Day.

hand to give advice or simply enthuse with you. Naturally there is the opportunity to purchase, but there are also splendid rose gardens to wander around – and just to be surrounded by such fragrance is a pleasure in itself.

If from Cosford you turn north instead of south on the A41, you will pass under the motorway, after which a right turn will take you to **Boscobel House**. A splendid 17th century half-timbered building in its own right, Boscobel's finest hour was when it sheltered the fugitive future Charles II after his defeat at the Battle of Worcester. The king spent his daytime hours famously hiding in an oak tree while Parliamentarian troops prowled the ground beneath. A storm-battered but much-revered descendent of this 'Royal Oak' can still be seen today. The visit also includes the dairy and smithy of this one-time working farm, and possibly a guided tour of the house itself.

A mile down the road from Boscobel House, the ruins of **White Ladies Priory** lie beyond woodland at the side of the road. Only parts of the 12th century church remain – of the associated buildings once inhabited by the nuns (the 'white ladies'), nothing can be seen, nor is there any trace of the large timber-framed house that once stood alongside. White Ladies Priory goes back a long way, and legend has it that it was here that Queen Guinevere retired after the death of King Arthur.

The final visit in this part of Shropshire must be to **Weston Park**, a fine 17th century stately home whose extensive grounds straddle the county boundary, just to the north of Boscobel House. Weston has a history to match

A king in hiding

The Battle of Worcester, fought on 3rd September 1651, was the final conflict of the Civil War. The greater numbers of Cromwell's New Model Army soon had the Royalists fleeing for their lives, among them Charles II, who from that moment was a much-wanted man. Unfortunately he was also a very recognisable man, being 6ft 2inches tall (exceptional for the time) and very thick-set. Charles rode through the night and in the early hours arrived at the door of White Ladies Priory in the grounds of Boscobel House. There the servant George Penderel took care of him, giving him clothes and a haircut to disguise him, and hiding him in the woods until the cover of night should allow him to attempt a crossing of the Severn. That river was so heavily guarded that Charles returned, this time to Boscobel House – where he was obliged to pass the day in an oak tree before being transferred to a priest hole in the house itself. From Boscobel Charles was first smuggled to the port of Bristol, but finding no sea passage available, was subsequently moved on to the south coast. After 6 weeks on the run, an unsuspecting coal boat was engaged to take him from Shoreham to Fécamp, and Charles spent the next 9 years in exile before returning to claim his throne.

its sizeable character, and was in its time a great favourite of Prime Minister Disraeli. Today it is managed by a trust and in summertime offers regular guided tours of the house itself, with unlimited access to the formal gardens, walks and acres landscaped by Capability Brown. Children are treated to a miniature railway, woodland adventure playground and a yew maze, and naturally there are appropriate restaurant and bar facilities for all. Weston is more than worth a visit, but before setting off it is a good idea to check its calendar because it may be closed at times of special events. Anything from horse trials and fungi forays to weddings, business conferences and even a G8 summit (1998) may be taking place in this idyllic venue!

At Weston this journey through Shropshire must end. It is almost 50 miles along Telford's great Holyhead Road from our beginning at the Chirk aqueduct. A similar distance – although no single road – separates Whitchurch in the north from Ludlow in the south. Although not in the league of Somerset or North Yorkshire, Shropshire is nevertheless one of England's largest counties. And would you agree that it is also the most rural, varied, interesting and beautiful of them all?

RAF Museum, Cosford

Rose Garden at David Austin

The White Ladies Priory

Boscobel House

Places to Visit

Tourist Information Centres

Telford (The Shopping Centre):
☎ 01952 230032

Ironbridge (The Toll House):
☎ 01952 884391

Places of Interest

Telford

Town Park

Open every day. ☎ 01952 290240

Wonderland

Open Oct to Mar, weekends and school holidays only, 10.30am–4pm; Apr to Sept every day 10.30am–4pm (6pm weekends and school holidays). Weekends leading up to Christmas 10.30am–6pm.
☎ 01952 591633

Telford Steam Railway, Horsehay

Open Easter to Sept. Static viewing Sat, trains run Sun and Bank Holidays. First train approx. 11am, last approx. 5pm.
☎ 07765 858348

Wellington

Sunnycroft

Open mid-Mar to Oct, Mon, Fridays, Sat and Sun only 1–5pm (last entry 1 hour before closing).
☎ 01952 242884

Preston-on-the-Weald

Hoo Farm Animal Kingdom

Open every day except Mon, mid-Mar to early Sept 10am–6pm; early Sept to Nov 10am–5pm (last entry 1 hour before closing). Special events in Dec.
☎ 01952 677917

Lilleshall Abbey

Open Apr to Sept every day 10am–5pm.
☎ 01926 852078

Broseley

Benthall Hall

Open Easter to Sept Tue and Wed 2–5.30pm (Sun also, Jul, Aug, Sept).
☎ 01952 882159

Buildwas Abbey

Open Easter to Sept, Wed to Sun and Bank Holidays, 10am–5pm.
☎ 01952 433274

Coalbrookdale

Open Air Museum of Steel Sculpture

Open Mar to Nov, every day except Mon, 10am–5pm. Open Bank Holiday Mon.
Tel 01952 433152

Green Wood Centre

Open every day, summer 10am–5pm; winter 11am–4pm.
☎ 01952 432769

Royal Air Force Museum

Cosford. Open every day throughout the year (except over Christmas and one or two days in New Year). 10am–5pm (last admission).
☎ 01902 376200

David Austin Roses

Open 9am–5pm, seven days a week.
☎ 01902 376334

Boscobel House and the Royal Oak

Open Easter to Oct, Wed to Sun and Bank Holidays 10am–5pm.
☎ 01902 850244
www.english-heritage.org.uk/boscobel

Continued over page

Places to Visit

White Ladies Priory
Site always accessible

Weston Park
Because the Park hosts a number of special events opening times vary, and are best obtained from:
www.weston-park.com.
☎ 01952 852100

Take a Walk

* Four excellent walks (around 2 hours each) have been marked out in the Ercall Woods. Free leaflets are available at the entrance opposite the hotel on the Little Wenlock-Wellington road. As an alternative (or as an addition) you could climb the Wrekin (see text)
* Don't assume an urban area like Telford doesn't offer good walks! To see the best of both countryside and modern development, take the newly-developed 12-mile loop called the South Telford Way. Free leaflets are available from Spout Farm House at the entrance to Town Park, or from the Tourist Office in Ironbridge
* At Coalbrookdale, enter the woods opposite Holy Trinity Church (on Church Road) and follow signposts to the rotunda for that magnificent view of the gorge (the rotunda itself is sadly no longer there). For longer walks, get the leaflet Walk the Gorge from the Tourist Office.
* The Severn Way follows the right bank of the river throughout the length of the gorge.

On Your Bike

* Telford and Wrekin Borough Council have produced a map of cycle routes in urban Telford. It can be downloaded from www.shropshire.gov.uk/cycling.

* Cyclists (and walkers) can enjoy the Perry Way, the route of the former Shropshire Union Railway line between Wellington and Donnington

For the Family

* The imaginative playgrounds and grassy acres of Telford Town Park are absolutely free (unless you go on to Wonderland), as is the Air Force Museum at Cosford
* At the other end of the scale you will need to dig into the pocket for a day at Hoo Farm or Weston Park and even more deeply for a session at Enginuity or Blists Hill Victorian Town. Note that if you intend to take in both the latter two, it is very likely that your best bet will be a Family Passport. Check prices carefully (www.ironbridge.org.uk)
* Forget all the man-made entertainment and go and climb a mountain – i.e. The Wrekin. It should take you less than an hour to the summit and children enjoy the challenge of a steepish climb. A house half-way up doubles as a teashop on high days and holidays.

A Rainy Day?

* There's no problem in Ironbridge! Those ten museums should keep you dry for a week never mind a day. Even at Blists Hill you can enjoy the houses and shops, although families might think the fairground would be better in the sunshine.
* A whole day could easily be spent at Cosford. They even offer plans for visits of 'under 2 hours', and suggestions for those 'with more time'. Take an umbrella for walking between the hangars!
* Try the Ice Rink or the Ten-Pin Bowl at Telford.

Leisure Facilities and Events

Hotel, Bed and Breakfast and Self-catering accommodation is plentiful throughout Shropshire, as are camping and caravan sites. The very helpful website www.shropshiretourism.co.uk will enable you to access up-to-date information on just about everything that is available.

Local Tourist Information Centres (telephone numbers given at the end of each chapter) are also happy to send you information with regard to accommodation.

It would be utterly impossible to review even a fraction of all the excellent eating establishments available in such a food-orientated county as Shropshire. Those named below are simply a few that offer something particularly interesting or unusual.

Details of most golf courses in Shropshire can be found on www.shropshiregolf.com

Wetlands and Waterways – The North

A bite to eat

There are good tearooms in every town, but **Jones' Coffee House**, with branches at Whitchurch and at Market Drayton, must score highly for its imaginative range of beverages.

The Boathouse beside the Mere at Ellesmere (currently under restoration) offers good food in a unique setting – as does the lockside café at Grindley Brook.

The Inn at Grinshill is a large Georgian establishment renowned for its first class food, **The Bear at Hodnet** is a beamed 15th century coaching inn and the **Cottage Restaurant** at Tern Hill Farm is a great find in an unlikely location (beside a busy roundabout).

Canalside pubs include **Jack Mytton's** at Hindhead (Spanish bar in large garden), the **Narrowboat** on the Ellesmere-Whittington road (characterful interior), and the **Wharf Tavern** at Goldstone Wharf (on the Shropshire Union).

Leisure activities:

Swimming pools

Oswestry Leisure Centre
College Road
☎ 01691 659349

Ellesmere Swimming Pool
Elson Road
☎ 01691 622027

Whitchurch Swimming Centre
White Lion Meadow
☎ 01948 662187

Wem Swimming Centre
Bowen's Field
☎ 01939 232460

Market Drayton Swimming Centre
Phoenix Bank
☎ 01630 655177

Golf

Henlle Park Golf Course
Henlle Road, Gobowen, Oswestry
☎ 01691 670680

Mile End Golf Club
Shrewsbury Road, Oswestry
☎ 01691 671246

Oswestry Golf Club
Aston Park, Oswestry
☎ 01691 610448

Macdonald Hill Valley Golf Course
Tarporley Road, Whitchurch
☎ 01948 667700

Hawkstone Park Golf Course
Weston-under-Redcastle
☎. 01948 841700

Market Drayton Golf Club
Sutton
☎ 01630 652266

Horse Riding

Penycoed Riding Stables
Llynclys Hill, Oswestry (6 miles south)
☎ 01691 830608

Freshfields Equestrian Centre
Longford, Market Drayton
☎ 01630 652495

Fishing

Ellesmere
Fishing on The Mere. Day tickets from Countryside Office ☎ 01691 624448, or from the Meres Visitor Centre.

Llangollen and Shropshire Union Canals
Monthly or day permits can be obtained through the Waterway Wanderers Scheme, which has information on sections of canal not leased to angling clubs at any particular time. Contact the Service Manager, British Waterways ☎ 01606 723905

Markets

Oswestry: Wednesday and Saturday. Farmers' market (local produce) last Friday of the month
Ellesmere: Tuesday
Whitchurch: Friday. Farmers' market first Saturday of the month
Wem: Thursday. Farmers' market second Saturday of the month
Market Drayton: Wednesday and Saturday

Events

Oswestry Show
1st Saturday in August (local foods, crafts, businesses, etc.)

Ellesmere Regatta
2nd Sunday in July. ☎ 01691 624488

Ellesmere Festival
(markets, decorated boats, etc.) 2nd weekend in September. ☎ 01691 622981

Wem Sweet Pea Show
Thomas Adam School, 3rd weekend in July.
☎ 01948 840779

Market Drayton Carnival
Whitsun Bank Holiday

Shrewsbury and Around

A bite to eat

Shrewsbury abounds with good tea shops where you can also get a light lunch. Very popular are **The Gallery Tearooms** in Princess Street, where you might need to book a table (☎ 01743 355550) and **Oscar's Café Bar** in the Music Hall, where they can usually find you a corner.

Out of town, the teashop at **Battlefield Farm** serves good home-made fare including breakfasts, light lunches and cream teas.

Restaurants, brasseries, wine bars and pubs are similarly in plentiful supply. In a converted warehouse on Victoria Quay, **The Armoury** has an interesting open atmosphere (wooden floors and tables, lots of prints and paintings, even a 'library') and river views.

Very different and right at the heart of things is the cosy, beamed 16th century **Three Fishes** (on Fish Street).

Out of town, the **Mytton and Mermaid** opposite the entrance to Attingham Park serves good food – but then so does the National Trust restaurant in the Park itself.

Swimming Pools

The Quarry Swimming and Fitness Centre
Priory Road (in Quarry Park) ☎ 01743 236583

Golf Courses

Meole Brace Golf Club
Shrewsbury. ☎ 01743 364050

Horse Riding

Causeway Equestrian Centre
Causeway Wood Farm, Acton Burnell ☎ 01694 731436

Fishing

Cound Trout Fishery:
4 miles south of Shrewsbury (off A 458), 26 acre lake for fly fishing. ☎ 01743 761114
www.coundtroutfishery.com

Markets

Shrewsbury: Tuesday, Wednesday, Friday, Saturday and Sunday. Farmers' market 1st Friday of the month

Events

Darwin Festival
Shrewsbury (lectures, exhibitions, guided walks, children's workshops). Throughout February. ☎ 01743 281281
www.darwinshrewsbury.org

International Cartoon Festival
Shrewsbury (professional cartoonists from all over the world let loose on The Square and venues around). Weekend in mid-April.
☎ 01743 281200
www.shrewsburycartoonfestival.com

Dragon Boat Festival
Shrewsbury (colourful fancy dress rowing event on the Severn - for charity).
Last Sunday in June.
☎ 01743 354450

Shrewsbury Flower Show
Quarry Park (music and entertainment, as well as the blooms) Friday and Saturday in mid-August. ☎ 01743 234058
www.shrewsburyflowershow.org.uk

Shrewsbury Folk Festival
(Shrewsbury and West Midlands Showground, just west of station). Bank Holiday weekend in late August. ☎ 01746 768813
www.shrewsburyfolkfestival.co.uk

Shrewsbury International Street Theatre Festival
(various locations in the vicinity of the Square). Last weekend in August.
☎ 0796 3857594
www.shrewsburystreetfest.co.uk

Blue Remembered Hills

A bite to eat

Devotees of the very-English institution of afternoon tea should not miss out on award-winning **Rocke Cottage** at Clungunford. Another classic choice would be de **Greys at Ludlow** (black-and-white clad waitresses, tiered cake-stands). But the whole area abounds with excellent tea-shops, and Bishop's Castle and Clun in particular are disproportionately supplied for their size.

The Bottle and Glass in out-of-the-way Picklescott is a well-known gem – but it has only a few dining tables, so it is important to book, even out of season (☎ 01694 751345). Similarly excellent and off-the-beaten-track are the **Royal Oak** at Cardington and the Horseshoe at Bridges. Then there's the **Crown at Munslow** (better inside than out), the **Stiperstones Inn** (very welcoming), the *Sun at Corfton* (own brewery), the ancient **Talbot** at Much Wenlock and so many more.

Leisure Activities:

Swimming Pools

Bishop's Castle Leisure Centre
Brampton Road
☎ 01588 630243

Much Wenlock Leisure Centre
Farley Road
☎ 01952 727629

Church Stretton
St Laurence's Primary School Swimming Pool
☎ 01694 722682

Ludlow
South Shropshire Leisure Centre, Bromfield Road
☎ 01584 874620

Golf

Arscott Golf Course
Pontesbury
☎ 01743 860114

Ludlow Golf Club
Bromfield
☎ 01584 856285

Church Stretton Golf Club
☎ 01694 722281

Elm Lodge Golf Course
Fishmore, Ludlow
☎ 01584 872308

Horse Riding

Minsterley
Oakage Riding Centre
☎ 01743 791418

Ludlow
North Farm Riding Establishment, Whitcliffe
☎ 01584 872026
For DIY equestrian holidays, visit the website
www.marcheshorsetrails.co.uk

Bishop's Castle
(Lydbury North) Walcot Hall Stables
☎ 01588 680514

Hughley
Mill Farm Riding Centre
☎ 01746 785645

Fishing

Minsterley
Fly and Course fishing at Onny Vale Trout and Course Fishery, White Grit
☎ 01588 650521

Bishop's Castle (Lydbury North).
Lakes at Walcot Hall (a Georgian mansion designed and once owned by Clive of India).
☎ 01588 680570

Church Stretton
Course fishing at Middle Farm Pool, Betchcott. ☎. 01694 751232

Ludlow
Stretches of the Teme and Corve are controlled by Ludlow Angling Club. For tickets,
☎ 01584 876997 or call in at the Cliff Hotel, Dinham

Markets

Bishop's Castle: Friday. Farmers' market 3rd Saturday in the month. Flea and Collectors' market, 1st Saturday
Church Stretton: Thursday. Farmers' Market 2nd and 4th Friday
Craven Arms: Saturday. Farmers' Market 1st Saturday
Much Wenlock: Saturday. Farmers' market 1st and 3rd Friday in the month
Ludlow: Monday, Wednesday, Friday and Saturday. Farmers' market 2nd Thursday in the month

Events

Music at Leasowes Bank
Ratlinghope. A series of informal concerts held in a converted barn. Everything from jazz to chamber music including a specially commissioned piece each year. Early to mid-July.
☎ 01743 790769
www.leasowesmusicfestival.co.uk

Farmer Phil's Festival
Ratlinghope. Just a mile or so to the south of Leasowes Bank Farm, Farmer Phil at Near Gatten Farm invites bands of many kinds (folk/rock/Celtic/reggae) to the revolving stage he designed from a rotary milking unit. Stilt walkers, jugglers, street theatre, etc add to the family atmosphere. Friday and Saturday in Mid-August.
☎ 01588 650459
www.farmerphilsfestival.co.uk

Bishop's Castle Michaelmas Fair
(includes procession of vintage cars and tractors – and some steamers). Weekend in late September.
☎ 01588 638154
www.michaelmasfair.org.uk

Church Stretton and South Shropshire Arts Festival
(music, drama, lectures, exhibitions). Latter half of July.
☎ 01694 723133
www.strettonfestival.org

The National Trust
Stages a comprehensive series of events on the Long Mynd (observing birds, butterflies, fungi, orienteering, star gazing, etc.).
☎ 01694 724536
www.cardingmillvalley.org.uk

Wenlock Olympian Games
Mid-July.
☎ 01952 727907
www.wenlock-olympian-society.org.uk

Festival at the Edge
(Stokes Barn, Much Wenlock). Long-established storytelling festival including music, comedy, poetry. 3rd weekend in July. Camping on site.
☎ 01939 236626
www.festivalattheedge.org

Clun Green Man Festival
1st weekend in May.
☎ 01588 640305
www.clungreenman.org.uk

Ludlow Festival
(Shakespeare in the Castle, talks, chamber music, opera, walks, ballet and the rest). 2 weeks June/July.
☎ 01584 872150
www.ludlowfestival.co.uk

Ludlow Food and Drink Festival
A great weekend for gourmets (taste the puddings, follow an 'Ale Trail', vote on the town's sausages, etc). Mid-September.
☎ 01584 873957
www.foodfestival.co.uk

From the Highest Hills to the Banks of the Severn

A bite to eat

If you are on Clee Hill, don't miss the unique **Craven Place Café and Tearoom** (see text). Bridgnorth has many restaurants for a light meal, but **The Quays** also offers a flower-decked patio overlooking the river.

Out of town there are more home-made cakes at the **Visitor Centre in Severn Valley Park** (they also make up fresh sandwiches to your requirements), and at **Dudmaston Hall** (same opening times as the Gardens, but you don't pay to access the tea shop).

The Crown at Hopton Wafers (16th century, stream and duckpond in garden), the **Bull's Head** at Chelmarsh (18th century, friendly), the **Railwayman's Arms** at Bridgnorth (on the Severn Valley Railway station), the Road and Rail at Hampton Loade (big garden, by the ferry crossing), the **Kremlin** at Clee Hill (Shropshire's highest pub - views) and the **Dog at Worfield** (pretty, in pretty village) are among many with something special to offer.

For something very special, **The Mill** at Alveley offers haute cuisine in a waterside restaurant overlooking pool and gardens.

Leisure Activities:

Swimming Pools

Bridgnorth Sports and Leisure Centre
Cliff Road ☎ 01746 761541

Golf Courses

Cleobury Mortimer Golf Course
(1 ½ miles north) ☎ 01299 271112

Bridgnorth Golf Course
(1 mile from centre) ☎ 01746 763315

Horse Riding

Hook Farm Equestrian Centre
Bridgnorth
☎ 01746 762872

Broad Acre
Bridgnorth
☎ 01746 781019

Fishing

Hurst Farm Lakes, Morville
Coarse and fly fishing.
☎ 01746 861219
www.holidayfishing.co.uk

Kingsnordley Fisheries
(5 miles south of Bridgnorth). Lakes for coarse fishing.
☎ 01746 781215

Shatterford Lakes
(on county boundary). Trout and coarse fishing.
☎ 01299 861597
www.shatterford.com

Markets

Bridgnorth: Street Market on Saturday. General Market under the Town Hall on Fridays and Saturdays. Craft Market on summer Sundays.

Events

Burwarton Show

(Classic agricultural show with lots of side stalls and family entertainment). Thursday in mid-August. ☎ 01746 787535 www.burwartonshow.co.uk

*Bridgnorth Music Festival

(rock, folk, jazz, etc.) Various venues around town. Last week of August.
☎ 01746 862240 www.bridgnorthmusicfest.com

Bridgnorth Jazz Festival

Hotels, inns etc around town. Last weekend in October. ☎ 01746 765737
www.bridgnorthjazzfestival.co.uk

Telford, Ironbridge and the East

A bite to eat

Ironbridge is very well endowed with excellent tearooms, most of them in the immediate vicinity of the Iron Bridge. Of the museums, **Blists Hill**, **Jackfield Tile Museum** and the **Museum of Iron** have refreshment facilities. Away from the Gorge, try **Flapjacks at Wellington**. Concealed in a humble back street (from the swimming pool, up Tan Bank and straight on), it offers superb lunches and most delectable cakes at more-than-reasonable prices.

The main road beside the river at Ironbridge (**The Wharfage**) offers a selection of interesting pubs. Choose between the **Malthouse** (large, with jazz bar and more formal restaurant), the **White Hart** (traditional inn gone modern, river views) and the **Swan** (great variety of food, intimate restaurant). Add to that the historically interesting **Tontine Hotel** and an upmarket wine bar in the High Street appealingly or otherwise entitled '**It's all about me**'. Elsewhere in the Gorge, try the cheerful **Golden Ball** (signed off road to Madeley) or, across the footbridge at Coalport, the riverside **Boat Inn** (good fresh home-made food – also famous for its flood levels!)

Leisure Activities:

Swimming Pools

Wellington Civic and Leisure Centre
Larkin Way, Tan Bank. ☎ 01952 382720

Oakengates Leisure Centre
New Road, Wrockwardine Wood. ☎ 01952 382810

Madeley Court Sports Centre
Court Street, Madeley. ☎ 01952 382770

Newport Swimming Pool
Victoria Park. ☎ 01952 380001

Telford Ice Rink

St Quentin Gate
Town Centre. ☎ 0845 1559966

Golf Courses

Telford Golf Course
Sutton Heights (near Coalport). ☎ 01952429977

The Shropshire Golf Course
Granville Park, Muxton (near Donnington). ☎ 01952 677800

Shifnal Golf Course
(1 mile north). ☎ 01952 460330

Patshull Park Golf Course
Near Pattingham (mid-way between Telford and Wolverhampton). ☎ 01902 700100

Horse Riding

Telford Equestrian Centre
Near Donnington. ☎ 0705 3532770

Fishing

Patshull Park Fisheries
Near Pattingham (see Golf Courses). Trout, coarse, pike.
☎ 01902 700774

The Monument Carp Fishery
Shifnal. ☎ 01952 462702

Markets

Telford: Friday and Saturday
Shifnal: Wednesday

Events

Wellington Literary Festival
Talks, workshops, drama, films, etc. Held at various venues throughout the month of October.
☎ 01952 567697 www.wellington-shropshire.gov.uk

British Falconry Fair
Chetwynd Park, Newport. Falconry displays, crafts, gundogs, ferrets, archery, quad bikes.
Early May Bank Holiday weekend. ☎ 01588 672708 www.countryfairs.info/ffcontact.html

Ironbridge Gorge World Heritage Festival
Open air entertainment, street market, music, heritage walks and more. Weekend in late
September. ☎ 01952 254959 www.ironbridgeheriagefestival.co.uk

Ironbridge Coracle Regatta
Sprint races, coracle polo etc – even a few coracles for you to have a go yourself. Dale End
Park, Coalbrookdale. August Bank Holiday Monday. Run by the Green Wood Centre.
☎ 01952 432769 www.greenwoodcentre.org.uk
The Green Wood Centre also organise an 'Apple Day' in mid-October – details on their
website.

Cosford Air Show
Sunday in mid-June. ☎ 01902 377922 www.cosfordairshow.co.uk

Midland Game and Country Sports Fair
Clay pigeon, fishing, gundogs, falconry, etc. Weston Park. Weekend in late September.
☎ 0845 23051

Index

Published in the UK by
Landmark Publishing Ltd
The Oaks, Moor Farm Road West, Ashbourne, DE6 1HD
☎ (01335) 347349 Fax: (01335) 347303
website: www.landmarkpublishing.co.uk

1st Edition
13 ISBN: 978-1-84306-441-1

Print: Gutenberg Press Malta
Design: Michelle Prost
Cartography: Jonathan Young

Front cover: St Alkmund's Place, Shrewsbury
Back cover, top: Rose Garden at David Austin
Back cover, middle: Moreton Corbet Castle
Back cover, bottom: The Wrekin from Grinshill
Back cover, right: Dancers at the Clun Festival

All images have been supplied by the author.